Mastering the Craft of Compelling Storytelling

Praise for Mastering the Craft of Compelling Storytelling

From Tess Gerritsen, bestselling author of *Die Again:*

> "Whether you're writing your first novel or your twentieth, this book is a must-have for any novelist. And it's one of the most readable, entertaining books on writing out there."

Laura Abbott, co-owner & managing editor, Amber Quill Press:

> "I've read many manuscript submissions that were near-misses. If those writers had had the benefit of this book, they'd be published right now. This is a must-read for the burgeoning storyteller and serious novelist, and it's a necessity for editors who seek to nurture their writing clients."

Dan Conaway, literary agent, Writer's House:

> "Learn the critical art of ruthless and rigorous self-editing from a man who understands the art better than most. His practical, sensible advice really can help you become a better writer."

Lou Aronica, editor, publisher, president of The Fiction Studio:

> "Writers will learn a great deal from the pages of this book. Rhamey offers the kind of advice that could make a huge difference in a writer's prospects."

Mastering the Craft of Compelling Storytelling

Ray Rhamey

FtQ
Press

Ashland, Oregon

ISBN 978-0-9909282-0-1

Library of Congress Control Number: 2014918781

Book cover and interior design by Ray Rhamey

Elegant quill art on title pages by Janis McCallen

Disclosure: much of the content of this book initially appeared as *Flogging the Quill, Crafting a Novel that Sells*, 2009, by this author. The original content has been expanded to deliver even more help for writers.

B.C. WRITER

BY RAY RHAMEY

As if rejection weren't enough.

This book is dedicated to writers who brave the steep and never-ending learning curve for writing novels and memoirs, striving to learn and improve.

It's a thank-you to the writers I've worked with in critique groups who have helped me with my own writing and in learning how to coach writers to strengthen story shortcomings.

And the biggest thank-you goes to my wife, Sarah, who has been a patient listener for, well, all the important times and many not so consequential—the companion of my life.

Contents

From Page to Head, Compellingly

DONALD MAASS, literary agent representing more than 100 novelists, author, teacher, blogger, analyst, and fiction expert says this about what's in *Mastering the Craft of Compelling Storytelling*:

> "Ray makes you think about what you are putting
> down on the page."

That might seem to be *de rigueur* and of little import, perhaps even damning with faint praise . . . but when it comes to the craft of compelling storytelling, it's what's on the page—and *only* what's on the page—that gets your story into your readers' heads.

Maybe.

And even if it does, will they turn the page?

And then *keep* reading?

There's the rub.

To achieve a page-turner (in the literal sense; no turning the page, no reading the book), you have to think about and deal with many aspects of what you put on the page. I take Don's assessment as a high compliment from a pro.

Wait a minute, you might say, I'm a good writer, I have a knack for prose. Perhaps you're even published in one way or another. You put good stuff on the page.

As literary agent Kristin Nelson says,

> "I think writers assume that good writing is
> enough. Well, it's not."

Ouch.

On her blog, *Agent in the Middle*, veteran literary agent Lori
Perkins says this:

> "Your novel has to grab me by the first page,
> which is why I can reject you on page one."

Some are even quicker than that. Dan Conaway, an executive
editor turned literary agent at Writers House, says:

> "I know most of what I need to know about a
> writer's chops in about a line and a half."

Again, ouch.

On the editorial side, Chuck Adams, Executive Editor of
Algonquin Books, put it this way:

> "You can usually tell after a paragraph—a page,
> certainly—whether or not you're going to get
> hooked."

Okay, you might say, but those are literary agents and editors
who see hundreds of submissions. They've got calluses on their
frontal lobes and it takes a bludgeon to hook them, but I'm an
Indie author. I'm going to publish myself, so I don't need to worry
about what they think. I'll appeal directly to readers.

Oh, will you? If you think literary agents and editors are
tough, wait until a reader squints at your first page with taking

money out of their pocket on the line. Sol Stein, publisher-editor-author-playwright, writes in *Stein on Writing* of his observations in a bookstore:

> "In the fiction section, the most common pattern was for the browser to read the front flap of the book's jacket and then go to page one. No browser went beyond page three before either taking the book to the cashier or putting it down and picking up another to sample."

I'll wager you have even less time on Amazon.com or another online bookseller where you're one swift click away from goodbye.

What did those bookstore browsers see in the novels they chose to purchase, and what did they fail to see in the rejects?

Were the rejects missing fulsome description?

Great dialogue?

Fascinating characters?

Deep themes?

Nope. Just one thing.

STORY

Bookstore and website browsers of novels and memoirs—and agents and editors—either see *immediate* signs of a story they want to read, or they do not. They either feel compelled to keep reading, or they do not. As quickly as within a single page.

You do it too, don't you?

It's not like when you ask a family member, or a friend, or even a critique partner to read your new novel—they have to read your stuff, and their responses are colored by knowing you. It doesn't get tough until you're asking someone to pay for your novel or memoir—a purchase by a reader, an agent spending her time and reputation by offering your book, or an editor gambling on the cost to print and market it.

To move your book toward the cash register, to generate a request by an agent for the full manuscript, or to make it to an editorial meeting by an acquisitions editor, you need to kick-start your story, sentence by sentence, on your opening page.

And then you have to keep the pages turning

Are you starting to think about what you're putting on your pages?

On my blog, *Flogging the Quill,* I've critiqued first chapters and prologues submitted by, at this writing, more than 800 aspiring novelists and memoirists. My challenge to these writers is to craft a first page that *compels* me to turn the page and read more. Page-turns by me and many of my readers are few and far between.

I also teach a workshop at writers' conferences called "Crafting a Killer First Page." In the workshop we read a first page and then the class votes on whether or not they would turn the page. The percentage of "no" votes goes up as they read more and more pages and see what doesn't work. One workshopper whose first page came up at the middle of the class told me later that he voted against his own work because of what he'd learned by the time we got to it.

To define "compel:"

> com • pel
>> verb
>> a. to force
>> b. to urge irresistibly

But do you really need to *compel*? Remember what Lori Perkins said:

> "Your novel has to grab me by the first page,
> which is why I can reject you on page one."

Or, as Donald Maass says in his book, *Writing the Breakout Novel,*

> "To hold our attention, a novel's action needs to compel us to read every word."

There's that word again. And when Donald is talking about a novel's action, it is your storytelling and only your storytelling that can deliver the ability for your narrative to compel.

It's what you put on the page.

So here's what I'm going to deal with in this book to help you think about what you're putting there in ways to make it not only deliver your story and your characters, but in ways that keep the reader reading.

SECTION 1: WORDCRAFT

We'll start at the granular level—your word choices and the ways in which you use them. Just as a painter must master mixing hues to achieve the desired effect, writers need to hone their ability to mix and order words to write for effect.

Some might think spending time on words is beneath their level of ability—to that I'll let bestselling thriller author M.J. Rose respond with her view of the coaching you'll encounter:

> "It reminds me of important things about fiction writing."

Or, as author Pete Barber, *NanoStrike,* says:

> "I still skim through 'Mastering the Craft' before I undertake a major edit. It helps to remind me about the basics—first learned and easiest forgotten."

You'll find the wordcraft section useful if you haven't thought about how these words can weaken your narrative:

- present participles
- without
- some
- very
- of
- eyes
- started
- with
- as

Section 2: Technique

There are tools of your trade akin to the brushes and palette knives of a painter.

Storytelling techniques. The "telling/showing" paradigm demystified; dealing with point of view (POV); transitions; flashbacks; avoiding overwriting; and more.

Description techniques. I'll show you how to create description that not only describes but characterizes—you'll use *experiential description* to do more than snapshot a scene. I'll cover describing point-of-view characters without breaking POV; how filters distance your reader; shooting yourself in the descriptive foot when it comes to action; how "conclusion" words fail in description; avoiding the lure of overwriting; and more. You'll gain a new insight into adverbs that can enhance description—adverbs are frequently a no-no, but I've found a use that is definitely a yes-yes.

Dialogue techniques. The use—and non-use—of dialogue tags; the technique of "beats" to deliver a character's experience, action, and character; how to use one of the most revealing kinds of dialogue, internal monologue; and delivering the sound of speech.

SECTION 3: STORY.

Vital story elements; a first-page checklist; strategies and methods for launching a story; creating tension, characters that readers connect with, story questions, really good bad guys, dimension in characters, and more.

WORKOUTS

Finally, you'll go to work in exercises where you apply the techniques and insights you've gained to real first-page openings created by writers like you who submitted their work to my blog—I'll include my notes and the votes I gave them.

Benchmark—a pre-test

IN THE ELEVEN "WORKOUTS" at the end of this book, I ask you to apply the coaching herein to samples sent to me by writers. Below is one of the examples you'll be working on, the opening of a novel sent to me by an Australian writer (note the British punctuation).

To create a benchmark for changes in how you perceive a narrative after reading this book, I suggest you read this excerpt now and decide whether or not you would turn the page.

Then evaluate its strengths and shortcomings, and think about how you would edit it and/or what comments you would give the writer to make it stronger. Then carry on. This is what would be the first sixteen lines on a manuscript's first page:

'Michael's gone!' Julia screamed into the payphone outside Flinders Street Train Station.'

'Calm down, Mrs Stewart. She'll be with you shortly.'

Julia bristled at the matter-of-factness of the receptionist's voice. 'I don't care if she's with the Queen. My husband is missing. I think I'm losing my mind.'

'Please hold and I'll see if I can interrupt.'

Click. Mozart replaced the receptionist's voice. The familiar hold music from the past sounded surreal against the background tram and traffic noise of the Melbourne thoroughfare.

A pedestrian bumped into her daughter's stroller, turning Shellie to tears.

'Stop that, you bad girl!' Julia rolled the stroller under the phone box, putting her child out of the way of the Friday afternoon commuters.

Shellie reached out and cried louder.

'Arrgghh!' Julia dropped the receiver, picked up the three year old and settled her on her hip. Shellie quieted, distracted now by an earring.

Ignoring her, Julia reached for the dangling receiver, and found silence. 'Hello? Hello!' *Don't be gone. I don't have any more change.*

'I thought I'd lost you.' The receptionist's cheerfulness was enough to piss off anyone.

Okay, now dive in.

Section 1: Wordcraft

Writing for effect

IF YOU WANT READERS to turn your pages, here's the *effect* you want your writing to have on them—to trigger in them the sights and sounds and smells and feelings and movement of what's happening in the story. Readers don't want approximations, they want the story's reality. They should *experience* the story, not just learn about what happens. And by "experience the story" I mean experience the *character's* story.

Memoirist and writing teacher Sheila Bender, *A New Theology: Turning to Poetry in a Time of Grief*, talks about writing a memoir in such a way that the reader becomes you. I think the thing to strive for in fiction is for your reader to become the character(s).

I call it *writing for effect*, the root of compelling storytelling. It's your writing craft that empowers your storytelling to sink its fingers into readers' imaginations and compel them to want to know what happens next.

Writing for effect is the core craft principle underlying my approach to creating an irresistible fiction narrative that immerses a reader in the experience of the story.

It's the lens through which I critique narrative in an edit and strive to view my own writing.

It's the objective that informs the coaching on storytelling, dialogue, description, and technique in this book.

It's knowing how to show and when to tell. It's why adverbs are often weak writing—and sometimes just the opposite, creators of nuance and subtlety that evoke a character's reality.

Writing for effect is the guiding light that can show you the way to a stronger story, and the searchlight that can illuminate shortcomings in your manuscript.

Failure to write for effect is why too many writers, especially beginning authors, do little more than put information on the page and end up with a report with a plot, not a novel or memoir.

In storytelling, you're not writing to inform the reader—you deliver information, of course, but that's not the purpose—you're writing to affect the reader. To craft narrative that creates an effect in the reader's mind—the experience of the story.

BASICALLY, IT'S ALL ABOUT STIMULUS/RESPONSE.

Maybe it's the psychology major in me, but I can't help but think of the stimulus/response paradigm. Pavlov taught dogs to expect food when he rang a bell, and thereafter the dogs salivated at the sound of that bell.

The reader provides the response to the words you use, visualizing a scene or seeing an action or experiencing a character or, even better, *feeling* an emotion. To complicate matters, there's a reader element involved that you can't make go your way—the reader's personal knowledge, filters, and baggage. A dog not trained to associate feeding with a bell won't salivate at the sound of one. The word "cat" has a different effect on a cat lover than it does on a cat hater. You can't control that, but you can still load your narrative gun with the best possible ammo. In practice, the workings of stimulus/response aren't simple, but they are the keys to writing for effect, and understanding that can open the door to successful storytelling.

You begin a story with a single stimulus—a word. Here's one now:

Vladimir's

With the exception of verbs, most words can't do much by themselves, so you string words into a sentence that forms a different stimulus.

> Vladimir's blade cut Johnson's throat, and Vladimir smiled.

Change the words and the *effect* is different.

> Vladimir's blade sliced open Johnson's throat, and Vladimir smiled.

To my mind, *sliced open* is far more visually evocative than *cut*. Another part of the effect here is to characterize Vladimir—for some reason, he enjoyed slicing open a man's throat. And this sentence raises story questions: Why did he slice the throat, and why did he smile? Is he a good guy or a bad guy?

All that from just one sentence of nine words.

Although we're writing for effect and the accumulating stimuli produce a dramatic portrayal of what's happening, we haven't yet reached the level of delivering the experience of the story. That experience comes through the character.

Vladimir is the point-of-view character, but this narrative is objective so far, shallow, a camera's view. Novels provide a unique way to create an experience—going deeper to show what's happening in a character's mind.

> Vladimir's blade sliced open Johnson's throat. The child-killer toppled, hands clutching his neck, blood flowing between his fingers. Vladimir watched him writhe and then become still. The bittersweet taste of vengeance filled Vladimir, and he smiled.

Your sentences accrue and, done well, coalesce into a greater stimulus—the story. The final result, the effect on your reader, begins with the word choices you make and how you put them together.

Adverbs: Good? Bad? Yes.

PERHAPS YOU'VE HEARD the view that you shouldn't use adverbs—bestselling author Elmore Leonard was dead set against them. Mostly, I agree. You should pitilessly weed out many of the adverbs that lurk in your manuscript because they are telling posing as showing.

Here's a simple-minded example of why adverbs can be the bane of writing for effect. A story starts with this:

> Jimmy walked slowly across the cluttered room.

Simple information. I see, fuzzily, a guy walking. Not very fast (but I can't really picture it). There's stuff in the room (but who knows what).

The effect? Not much. No clear picture comes to mind. First thing to do: ditch the verb/adverb combo and choose a verb that evokes a picture, at the least, and at best characterizes the action. If, for example, your story is suspense, then how about . . .

> Jimmy *crept* across the cluttered room.

Better. Following are other variations, depending on the nature of the story:

In a fight scene, Jimmy would have *lunged* across the room.
If Jimmy is a dancer, then he *glided.*
Make Jimmy a burglar and he *skulked.*
If Jimmy is in no hurry, then he *ambled.*
If Jimmy is in a hurry, then he *dashed.*
If Jimmy has been over-served at a bar, then he *weaved.*
Or maybe he *tottered,* or *staggered,* or *lurched,* or, my personal favorite, *sloshed.*

Each of those verbs evokes a picture of Jimmy's body moving in specific ways. They are "visual" verbs that created a specific effect in your mind.

Stimulus > response.

There's another bit of lazy writing in the example sentence— the adjective "cluttered." It did nothing to create a picture. At the very least, we should see what the room was cluttered with, e.g.:

> Jimmy crept across a room cluttered with shrunken heads.

Ooooo. See how specificity stirs up story questions? Don't you want more? What about the room? Is it dark? Any smells? Sounds? Is anyone else there? What about characterization? Put on Jimmy's skin and . . .

> He was glad that the light of his candle was dim—all those tiny faces staring up at him were entirely too creepy. He set a foot down and winced at a crunch. He froze, listening for sounds of renewed pursuit. But only the scurrying of rats troubled the air, musty with the dust of the dead.
> Rats?
> Oh, fine.

Back to adverbs. There's a reason adverbs rob you of effect.

ADVERBS ARE TELLING

I believe that adverbs that modify action verbs are merely a form of telling. They are abstractions of action, pallid substitutes for the real thing, mere stand-ins for showing. In a sense, they are "conclusion" words. As a result, they rarely give the reader much of an experience.

For example, one of my clients wrote,

> She grinned mischievously.

The adverb tries to tell us the nature of the grin. Now, the average reader would probably plug in some sort of vague image of a grin, keep on rolling, and never realize she had been cheated—but she was. There's a much more lively and concrete picture to be created in the reader's mind. For example:

> She grinned, mischief sparking in her eyes.

In the original, because you have to interpret "mischievously" (what, exactly, is that?) the effect is to evoke an unsure image of a grin. In the second, you see a face in action: lips curve, you see a grin, you see eyes, you see playful activity behind those eyes. All that from four extra words chosen for effect.

Or, hey, what about something like this . . .

> She grinned like a fox that had just found the
> key to the henhouse.

The example above goes beyond word choice to use a simile that taps into meaning and characterization greater than a simple visual.

In writing this, I decided to check my manuscripts for adverbs and soon spotted one posing as description. Here's the sentence:

> She saw Murphy, like a big, round boulder parting a stream of girly secretaries cramming in a buzz of noontime shopping—except this boulder stared blatantly at their bobbing chests as they passed.

"Stared blatantly?" Definitely another case of making an adverb try to do the work of real description—it's telling me the nature, the effect, of the stare, not showing it. To be fair, this was from my first novel, written several years ago, on the lower slopes of my learning curve.

In this case the answer lay, as usual, in the verb. I swapped out "stared blatantly" for "leered." Much better, giving a clear picture with fewer words and adding semantic overtones. While I was at it, I tightened the sentence a little, too:

> She saw Murphy, like a big, round boulder parting a stream of girly secretaries cramming in a buzz of noontime shopping, leering at their bobbing chests.

WATCH OUT FOR ADVERBS IN DIALOGUE TAGS

Many writers use adverbs to explain dialogue rather than show how the dialogue is delivered. For example:

> "This is my dialogue," he said hesitantly.

That's lazy use of an adverb. You could say this . . .

> He hesitated, then said, "This is my dialogue."

But that's not precisely what "said hesitantly" means, is it? It suggests a hesitation somewhere in the speech. Wouldn't it be more effective if we *dramatized* the hesitation so the reader actually experiences a pause rather than reads about one?

> "This . . ." He swallowed and glanced at her face.
> ". . . is my dialogue."

Go on an adverb hunt in your manuscript and replace them with the action they only hint at and you'll be writing for effect.

I DISCOVER THAT NOT ALL ADVERBS ARE BAD GUYS

When doing my manuscript check, I came upon a pair of adverbs in one sentence . . .

> He found Emmaline to be annoyingly cheerful
> but pleasingly proficient.

But these adverbs worked for me. Wait, I thought, how come they feel right when I've preached loud and long to avoid adverbs? Then I realized that they modified adjectives rather than verbs. Aha!

GOOD CHOLESTEROL AND BAD CHOLESTEROL

There was a time we were told that all cholesterol was bad. Then we learned that there is good cholesterol and bad cholesterol.

Well, I changed my position that all adverbs are suspect, if not bad. I think there are "good" adverbs, story-friendly adverbs that add just the right flavor to an adjective, enhancing it with a more complete shade of meaning.

Consider the sentence describing Emmaline. Could I have achieved what I wanted, which was to give insight into one character's feeling and attitudes toward another, without the adverbs?

He found Emmaline to be cheerful but proficient.

Nope. I've lost how the viewpoint character feels about Emmaline as *annoyingly* cheerful and *pleasingly* proficient—these two adverbs characterize the point-of-view character as a curmudgeon who is capable of being positive as well. And without them the "but" has to become "and" because the contrast is lost.

I went on a search for other adverbs and found . . .

> Her fair cheeks fetchingly reddened by the cold,
> she looked no older than a teenager.

Yep, for me this works. It would have been okay to write . . .

> Her fair cheeks reddened by the cold, she looked
> no older than a teenager.

. . . and you would have gotten a picture. But take "fetchingly" out and you lose the point-of-view character's internal response to the girl's coloring. With the addition of the adverb to this adjective, you also get the character's experience, i.e. his emotional reaction to the appearance he sees—fetching, attractive.

The pattern I was discovering seemed to be that adverbs are a positive addition when coupled to adjectives in order to add a point-of-view character's nuance to what would otherwise be simple description. Another instance from the same manuscript:

> He loved the Staffordshire blue-and-white rose
> pattern, beautifully detailed and botanically
> accurate right down to the thorns on the stems.

Take "beautifully" and "botanically" out of that sentence and I think it loses both meaning and flavor. One more:

> She changed her disguise to the queenly dignity
> of a white-haired society matron she'd met in
> Brussels.

To "show" the quality of her dignity without the adverb would have required something like this:

> She changed her disguise to that of a dignified,
> white-haired society matron she'd met in Brus-
> sels who'd had the manner of a queen.

Not as effective, is it? "Queenly" adds an element of royalty and all that goes with it to the woman's appearance to signal a great deal to the reader—erect posture, chin up, perhaps an aloof gaze, a look of being in charge—with just one word.

Here's an example taken from a client's manuscript of a good adverb and bad adverb in the same sentence:

> A young waiter with carefully streaked hair
> smiled suggestively at her.

For me, the first adverb expands the waiter's character by giving a sense of precision and extra care taken in the arrangement of the streaks, which tells me something about him as well. But I'd like to see the second adverb replaced with something more truly pictorial.

When you go hunting for adverbs, it's when they modify action that you should consider looking for a better verb to do the job, and when they amplify adjectives that you may find adverbs to be good cholesterol.

Similarly, keep an eye out for instances where an adjective can be enhanced by an adverb to characterize the point-of-view character.

Weed out weak, wasted and wrong words

A PUBLISHING HOUSE ACQUISITIONS EDITOR once said, "Most of what we get should never have left the writer's hand."

Every word counts—a cliché, a truth. Reading and imagining and experiencing a narrative is a cumulative process. Meanings and usage add up, bit by bit, into gestalts that insert what's happening to the character into your reader's mind.

Wrong words, words used in an incorrect way, confuse your reader and take them out of the story, not to mention costing you credibility and suspension of belief. Yet the manuscripts of novice writers are filled with just that.

Weak words fail to deliver vivid pictures and actions—do you want that? Waste words take up space and slow the pace—and are among the first discouraging things a professional spots.

Here are some of the worst offenders.

-ING

Let's start with half a word. "Inging," over-use of the present participle, frequently slows pace and mushes meaning. More often than not, "ings" should be "eds" for crisp writing.

> She was polishing her glasses as she searched for
> the right words.

I think this is passive and slow to create a picture in the reader's mind. Much more to the point and quicker is:

> She polished her glasses as she searched for the right words.

Examples from other samples I've received follow; see how much crisper and more effective the sentences are when the participle is avoided.

> The rain was turning into snow as they drove.
> The rain turned into snow as they drove.

> Dylan was circling the cabin.
> Dylan circled the cabin.

> Joanne was hoping that she would get to see her family skiing.
> Joanne hoped she would get to see her family skiing.

> Bob was getting more and more nervous.
> Bob grew more and more nervous.

> "No," the heavy woman said, rummaging through the shopping bag she was carrying.
> "No," the heavy woman said, rummaging through the shopping bag she carried.

or, even crisper:

> "No," the heavy woman said, rummaging through her shopping bag.

There are times, though, when "ing" (for me) helps convey an ongoing process. For example, consider "Thinking of his face, she hesitated." versus "She thought of his face and hesitated." For me the first version puts a thoughtful look on the character's face and creates a pause in whatever she's doing, and the second version is just action.

In one of the examples above I left "skiing" because it was the ongoing action of her family that the character wanted to see.

SOME

A waste word, a verbal habit something like the "uh" many people use in speech. Several examples follow (I almost said "some," but that was so vague); see how cutting the "somes" costs nothing yet makes the sentence crisper.

Married women always wore ~~some~~ bangles around both their wrists.

Do you have ~~some~~ pressing business?

My big band attained ~~some~~ modest local fame and national press.

There was ~~some~~ movement as the crocodiles attempted to steer clear.

She had ~~some~~ packing to do.

~~Some~~ tantalizing smells were wafting towards them from across the river. *(and let's change were wafting to wafted)*

He had to have ~~some~~ new tires installed.

VERY

Another waste word. Here's Mark Twain's advice:

> "Substitute 'damn' every time you're inclined to write 'very'; your editor will delete it and the writing will be just as it should be."

Examples:

I want to have the ~~very~~ best students. *(redundant—best is best)*

Mr. Simpson has been ~~very~~ eager to meet you. *(there are no degrees of eagerness—redundant)*

. . . in the ~~very~~ coldest part of winter. *(redundant—coldest is coldest)*

They were ~~very~~ hungry. *(starving or famished are more specific, more effective)*

During lunch she becomes ~~very~~ quiet. *(redundant—quiet is quiet)*

OF

In my first novel a reader picked up on a habit I had of overusing "of" as in, "He emptied his pot of coffee." I used my word processor's search tool to hunt for "of" and found many that I could change to either a possessive or use an adjective, e.g., "He emptied his coffee pot." This may seem mindlessly simple to you, but I found lots of places to tighten my narrative, which helped with pace and clarity.

Do a search for "of"—in the search dialogue box, click the "More >>" button and select "Find whole words only."

EYES

Many writers use "eyes" when what they really mean is gaze, or glance, or stare. While I understand that readers will "get it," it's still an improper usage. Some examples from actual manuscripts in which I take the usage to the next logical step:

> Her eyes were on the floor. Luckily, no one stepped on them.

> His blue eyes bored into her. And then blood gushed from the two holes in her belly.

> She felt the woman's eyes searching for her. It tickled when they slid across her face.

> His tired eyes land on me as he glances around the room. Then they drop to the floor and roll under the couch.

> My eyes follow the headlights. I ignore the wrenching pain when they leave their sockets.

> Roger kept his eyes on the road. He realized his mistake when the ice cream truck ran over them.

SUDDENLY

Elmore Leonard said to never use "suddenly." Considering his success and mastery of the narrative art, that's good enough for me.

I suspect that writers may mean "unexpectedly" rather than suddenly. I can make a case for "unexpectedly," which goes to character, but with "suddenly" I say just insert the action and the reader will experience its suddenness in the same way the character does.

Fire up your word processor, open your manuscript, launch the search tool, and type these weak, wasted, or wrong words in the Find what: box and go hunting for opportunities to make your narrative stronger and sharper.

Don't get me started

A COMMON LOCUTION that I see in manuscripts (and published novels) is "started to." Also, "began to." While there are times when those expressions are appropriate, they aren't nearly as frequent as some writers seem to feel.

When/if you use "started to" and "began to" in your narrative, spend a moment and think about what the words really mean.

Here are some examples of "started to" drawn from a number of submissions.

> When we started to get repeat responses to stimuli, we changed the system.

This says that the two things happened simultaneously, although they couldn't have; they didn't change the system until after the repeat responses occurred. Rewrite:

> After we got repeat responses to the stimuli, we changed the system.

What about this one?

> She turned away and started to laugh.

What is the start of a laugh? "H—" and then silence? No, the character laughed. Rewrite:

> She turned away and laughed.

Tears make an appearance:

> Her tears started to flow.

So they appeared in the corners of her eyes and then just sat there? Nope, if they flowed at all, they rolled on down her cheeks. Rewrite:

> Her tears flowed.

Getting a character moving:

> Larry slid from his stool and started to follow the beggar.

So did Larry get his feet on the floor, lift a foot, and then stop? Take a step or two and stop? No, he followed the beggar. See how much crisper it is to say:

> Larry slid from his stool and followed the beggar.

Can an action be partial?

> He started to laugh but stopped short when he saw how angry she was.

Another "H—" here? Wouldn't the following create a better picture of what might really happen?

He laughed, but then stopped when he saw how
angry she was.

What about thoughts?

His mind started to whirl with crazy ideas.

So what's the idea here? His mind starts, like a song beginning, and then, "r-r-r-r," fades out? Not likely.

His mind whirled with crazy ideas.

Be careful of continuity.

She started to sob and Steve held the weeping
child in his arms.

Aren't starting a sob and actually weeping different?

She sobbed, and Steve held the weeping child
in his arms.

Actually, written this way, "weeping" isn't needed.

She sobbed, and Steve held the child in his arms.

Here's confusing mix of actions:

She began to back away when a faint movement
in the yard stopped her.

A really confusing set of words for me. She was backing and
a movement stopped her? Doesn't seem possible. Rewrite:

> She backed away, but then stopped when she saw movement in the yard.

Sometimes, though, "started" is right.

> She stopped him when he started to rise to his feet.

This one is okay because the action was interrupted.

WITH

Another usage that can tangle meaning is "with." It can befuddle your reader when it adds things together nonsensically. When you think about what the words really mean, there are times when "with" is the wrong word—and it's your job to think about what words really mean.

I've had writers disagree with me on this, so I checked the dictionary. In a long list of meanings for the preposition "with" as a function word, this was included: "as the doer, giver, or victim of." That's how my sense of language interprets it. For example:

> He watched her with a satisfied smile.

So his teeth are capable of vision? Maybe, in a sci-fi adventure, but most of us use our eyes for this sort of thing. The writer who disagreed with this said that in this case it simply means he had a satisfied smile while he watched her. While I will agree that most people would interpret it that way, the construction still means that it was the smile he used to watch her with.

Also, this is telling—what does a "satisfied smile" look like? Rewrite:

> He watched her and smiled, satisfied.

This one is one heck of a dog:

> The dog started to chase the sheep with a snarl.

A double whammy: first the "started to," and then how did the dog hold the snarl with which he chased the sheep? In his teeth? How does one use a snarl in a chase, anyway? Rewrite:

> The dog snarled and chased the sheep.

Misuse of roaring.

> With a roar of encouragement, the watchers
> pushed him back into the fight.

So how did they get a grip on the roar in order to push with it? Aren't those things slippery? Rewrite:

> The watchers roared encouragement and pushed
> him back into the fight.

A tragic use of "with."

> She ran into his arms with a strangled sob.

Where did she get the strangled sob? Who strangled the poor thing?

> Strangling a sob, she ran into his arms.

Here's a useful sound:

> Margaret straightened her back with a groan.

I never thought to use a groan to straighten my back. Rewrite:

> Margaret groaned when she straightened her
> back.

A touching use of "with."

> He touched the cat with a worried expression.

So did he place his face against the cat? Rewrite:

> Worried, he touched the cat and frowned.

Do a search for "started to" and "began to" and "with" and see if you find any of these potential confusers lurking in your narrative.

~~without~~

Do without "without"

I'LL WAGER YOU'VE SEEN one or more of these phrases in stories:

- Without a sound
- Without a glance
- Without a doubt
- Without a thought
- Without a word

You might even have used them. I have.

It seems to me that most of the time these phrases are about as useful as your appendix. They are comfortable-feeling collections of words that attempt to describe a negative, an absence. But I think they are frequently lazy writing. They are a missed opportunity to write for effect.

If whatever it is the story is doing without isn't there, why bring it up? You, the writer, control absolutely everything the character experiences. If you don't put something into the narrative, it doesn't exist, does it? So why tell the reader that what isn't there isn't there?

Actually, in most cases I think that the writer intends to create meaningful narrative, it's just that using "without" can leave the reader missing the sense of what's happening. Luckily, there are ways to rewrite "withouts" to create the right effect in a reader's mind.

Let's try doing without without in the following examples.

WITHOUT A SOUND

> He crossed the room without a sound.

You, the author, control what the reader "hears." If you don't supply a sound, there is none. In my view, here "without a sound" is redundant. Do you hear anything if the narrative says this?

> He crossed the room.

Nope. In this case the author probably wanted to indicate the stealthy nature of his movement. If so, don't do it with an absence, do it with something specific that evokes the character's intent.

> Stepping lightly to make no sound, he crossed the room.

But that's sorta telling, isn't it? And it uses an adverb for description. Why not show rather than tell? For example:

> He removed his shoes and tiptoed across the room in his socks.

Don't you automatically imagine his movement as being silent?

WITHOUT A GLANCE

> She picked up her bag and walked off without a backward glance.

Okay, that hints at something going on in the character, but only hints. Wouldn't it be better from a characterization point of view to do something such as:

> She picked up her bag and walked off, resisting the
> urge to look back, to see his face one more time.

WITHOUT A THOUGHT

> She made her decision without a second thought.

Sure, you'll tell me that the writer is trying to characterize here, that perhaps the character is impulsive. But why do it with an absence? Could it be more positively stated? For example:

> She plunged ahead and made her decision.

WITHOUT A WORD

> Alex stepped into the room without a word.

So he left it outside the room? Will he have go back and get it if he needs it? Which word? Why not just:

> Alex stepped into the room.

Here's another "without a word":

> Let's go," she breathed, excited and a little fright-
> ened. Without a word, they turned as one to go.

I think it's the "without a word" phrase that seems least likely to contribute. If you, the writer, don't put any words on the page for the character to say, then they weren't said. See how much crisper and more direct this is without without.

> "Let's go," she breathed, excited and a little frightened. They turned as one to go.

I can see, perhaps, trying to characterize an action by using "without." I think the following attempts to do that:

> Jessica scooped the mug up and marched off without a word.

But this could characterize better with something like:

> Jessica bit back a retort, scooped up the mug, and marched off.

There are times "without" is useful, of course. From a sample:

> She felt a twinge of regret that she would be leaving Loren without a word of goodbye.

By the way, avoid using "felt"—it's a filter that distances the reader from the character's experience, something we'll get into later. I think the above would be stronger if it were:

> She regretted that she would be leaving Loren without a word of goodbye.

I searched my books for "without a." In my first novel I found:

> She hung up without a goodbye, which suited him fine.

This seems to work because the absence of expected behavior is what the character notices.

> He sagged and left without a look back.

The "without a look back" got cut.

In novel number two I found a "without a glance back." I think it should be removed, although I was tempted . . .

I also found two uses of "without a word" that I immediately cut.

The third novel:

> Then Dudley said, without an ounce of his usual
> sarcasm, "I'm sure it is, pardner."

Seems to me the phrase works here to characterize the speech. If I took it out, you wouldn't get the tone, and it is the absence of sarcasm that counts. I think the construction also suggests that the recipient of this speech (the POV character) expects sarcasm from Dudley, which characterizes both of them.

I think that there are times when the absence of something can be meaningful. In the following example, someone is running a horse (Dusty) through a pasture.

> Ten feet from the gully's edge, without a hint of
> warning, Dusty turned at a right angle and raced
> away from the trench.

Ordinarily, a horse's behavior sends signals to a rider, especially about a significant change in direction. Mentioning the absence here lets us know that what happens next is totally unexpected and that the rider had no chance to brace for it. As a result, this happened:

Jesse left the saddle and flew straight ahead, riding air.

Here's another one:

A cigarette without a light is as useless as a kiss without a pucker.

When I searched novel number four, I found no instances of "without a." Good for me.

Without a qualm, I urge you to search your manuscripts for "without a".

Watch your as

WHAT'S WRONG WITH this bit of narrative?

> As I sipped my coffee this morning, I typed,
> "Watch your as."

Well, I'm not about to be physically able to sip my coffee and type simultaneously unless I've got three hands. Oh, I guess it's possible—if I were sipping my coffee through a long, long straw while typing. But who does that?

We're about to pick at a nit here—the misuse of the "as" construction. I suspect you've seen a phrase such as the example above and it may not have struck you that something was awry. When you examine it, though, it describes a highly improbable event.

Y'see, in this situation "as" means simultaneously. Often I see writers use "as" when they should be using "when" or "after."

In the opening example, it should be something such as:

> I sipped my coffee and then I typed, "Watch
> your as."

Following are examples collected from samples and manuscripts I've received.

> Morgan collapsed onto the sofa as his knees
> gave way.

To my mind, the collapse was the *result* of his knees giving way—it follows the giving way and isn't simultaneous. He wouldn't collapse as they gave way because they haven't finished giving way and thus are not collapsed. The fix here is to use "when" ("after" would also work):

> Morgan collapsed onto the sofa when his knees
> gave way.

What about this one?

> As I flipped the switch the kitchen was flooded
> with light and I saw Portia on the floor.

You see it coming, don't you? While I'm at it, I'll get rid of a "was."

> When I flipped the light switch, light flooded the
> kitchen and I saw Portia on the floor.

That was a clear case of "when" because light would not flood the kitchen until after the switch was flipped. With "as," the switch could be anywhere in the process of completing the circuit, including before it's completed.

"As" often ignores a stimulus and response scenario.

> George stiffened as the man swore a solemn oath.

I see the stiffening as a reaction to the nature and content of the oath, not the act of swearing it. How would George know it was solemn until it was spoken? An adjustment:

The man swore a solemn oath and George stiffened.

Some uses of "as" are downright sloppy:

Lee jokes as he swigs from his bottle.

Have you ever tried telling a joke while simultaneously taking a swig from a bottle? If that's your habit, remind me not to buy you a drink. How it might be written:

Lee swigs from his bottle and then jokes.

From a romance:

As their eyes met her knees turned to butter.

Nope, the buttery knees were a reaction to the meeting of their gazes (not eyes). "When" shows you the sequence of events.

When their gazes met, her knees turned to butter.

From horror:

Chills ran down Tim's spine as he realized that evil was close to his son.

Once again, there's a cause-and-effect sequence necessary here. Doesn't it seem logical that the chills are caused by the realization and can't be running anywhere until after the realization?

When Tim realized that evil was close to his son, chills ran down his spine.

Here's one from a published writer:

> Instinct saved my face from being slashed as I
> ducked away at the last second.

Once again, we're dealing with a linear cause and effect. Seems to me that his instincts caused the ducking, and therefore had to precede it. The instinctive motivation to move and the movement itself can't be simultaneous. Here's one way to do it with a semi-colon:

> Instinct saved my face from being slashed; I
> ducked away at the last second.

Another cause-and-effect situation:

> Squirrels scattered as my bike tires hit the cinder
> alley behind our house.

Again, "when" seems to me to be the more accurate word. The squirrels react to the sound of the tires hitting the gravel, which can only be generated when they hit, and then the squirrels hear it. An ambivalent usage:

> He quivered as her feminine odor wafted into
> his nostrils.

This one is borderline. He could certainly do the quivering as the odor wafted in, but the writer's clear intent was to let the reader know that the odor caused the quiver. Rewrite:

> He quivered when her feminine odor wafted
> into his nostrils.

USING YOUR AS

There are, of course, times when the "as" construction serves a narrative well by describing things that can, and should, happen simultaneously. In these cases, "as" serves as a form of "while" to show how things are happening. For example,

> Marcie laughed as she swung Amy back and forth.

> As he lathered his face, he debated whether to wear a suit or not.

> She gnawed her lip in frustration as she watched him leave.

I suggest (and I've done this with my own work) doing a search for "as" (remember to select "Find whole words only" or it'll drive you crazy) and see if your usage truly makes sense.

Section 2: Technique

Once upon a . . .

STORYTELLING TECHNIQUES

IN WRITING A NOVEL, there are all kinds of things you have to know how to do. You need to know how to "show" a scene rather than "tell" it. On the other hand, there are times when "tell" is a better thing to do than "show." How's a writer to know?

And then there's point of view—first person, second person, deep and surface third person, omniscient. Shifting the point of view in a narrative can be a great technique or a crummy one, depending on when and how you do it.

Motivating an action or a scene sometimes calls for setting it up many pages sooner—how do you avoid *deus ex machina*?

You worry about pace, about keeping things moving . . . is there ever a time you should slow down? The answer is yes.

Unless you want to your reader to become confused or lost, transitions need to be smooth and clear. And what about slipping into the past to show a precursor to what's happening now?

This section covers:
- How to tell, when to show
- Point of view: a slippery slope
- Head-hopping as seen by an editor and an agent
- Story as garden
- Linger for involving storytelling
- From there to here, then to now
- Flashing back

When to tell, how to show

DAN CONAWAY, WRITERS HOUSE LITERARY AGENT and former executive editor at Penguin Putnam, had this to say about what I have to say about showing and telling:

> "While it'd be crazy to suggest that a writer's performance in the 'show don't tell' drill is what separates amateurs from Olympians, there's no doubt that internalizing Ray's wonderful encapsulation of the principle will improve the chances of a reader (like this grumpy editor, say) reading more than a single paragraph of your manuscript before tossing it on the scrap heap."

In a recent edit, I pointed out instances where I felt my client was telling versus showing. Even though I showed her ways to show what she had told, she said, "I'm still not sure I know how to 'show' rather than 'tell'."

I understand why. After all, we use the telling mode all the time in conversations with friends, and it works.

"I was really surprised."

"I was so pissed."

"I was incredibly happy."

WHEN TO TELL

There are times when telling is the right thing to do. It's when you need to summarize an event because using a scene would be wrong in terms of pace, tension, etc. A common example is when you've shown an event in an earlier scene and then the story comes to a place where your character needs to pass along what happened to another character. Rather than drag your reader blow by blow through something she already knows, summarize:

> April told May how June had told Julie where to shove her opinion.

That's a necessary and effective use of telling. There are other times when it's the best thing to do, too, when what needs to happen is so mundane that to waste words on it is to waste words. For example, a character is talking on his cell phone. When he finishes the conversation, you could "show" this:

> Bob pressed the little green phone icon on his cell phone to end the call.

Truly, that wasn't needed and smacks of overwriting. Instead:

> Bob ended the call.

The reader can easily imagine ending a call with a cell phone if they've ever used one, and, even if they haven't used one, they've seen it on television.

So what's so bad about a lot of telling in a novel? You "tell" a story, right? Not really. In a novel or memoir you dramatize with scenes. When you're writing for effect, you craft words that create a very specific result in the reader's mind, a vital sense of what is happening. You can only do that through showing.

Your readers want what they read to trigger in them the sights and sounds and smells of what's happening in the story. They don't want approximations, they don't want a report, they want to experience the story's reality.

How to show

You spot *telling* by looking for declarative sentences. The verb "to be" is often a sign of a telling statement. On the other hand, *showing* is using behavior (action, speech, thoughts) to *illustrate or dramatize* what the character is feeling/doing.

Here's *telling* versus *showing* from actual writing samples.

The scene: Anna is beat from a long, bad day at work and now she's spent hours at the hospital with her father, who has been unconscious for days. You want to give the reader Anna's physical and emotional condition. This author wrote:

> Anna was physically and mentally exhausted.

Sure, you get information. You have an intellectual understanding of her condition. But you have no sense of what Anna feels like, do you? To *show* that Anna is physically and mentally exhausted, you could write this:

> All Anna wanted to do was crawl into bed and go to sleep. But first she would cry. She didn't think she could be calm and composed for another minute.

The scene continues: Anna's father suddenly wakes and thrashes around wildly, gasping, making monitors go wild. You want to give the reader Anna's reaction. The author told us this:

> Anna was frightened.

She could have shown us with:

Oh, God, what was wrong with him? "Dad?"
Why didn't he respond? "Nurse, do something!"

Yes, it takes more words to *show* her fear, but remember that here you're not trying to inform the reader but to deliver an experience.

As you go through your manuscript, whenever you come across a declarative sentence that simply delivers information rather than shows behavior, you may have an instance of telling.

Unless it's a legitimate use of summary, your task is to visualize the character in that state or situation. See the movie. As the author, you can also "hear" thoughts. Show the reader the thinking or speaking or moving in a way that illustrates what the reader needs to know.

Another example of *telling* that deals with the use of adverbs.

Telling:
He stabbed the man furiously.

See how an adverb tells rather than shows?

Showing:
He plunged the dagger into the man's chest
again and again and again, screaming "Die!"
each time the blade stabbed into flesh.

One more example. Jesse has been working for hours under the Texas sun. We need to let the reader know how he feels.

Telling:
Jesse was very hot.

Seriously, I see descriptions like that in manuscripts all the time. How about this?

> *Showing:*
> Jesse felt like an overcooked chicken, his meat damn near ready to fall off his bones.

Now, that's hot. Another thing I often see is where a writer does a good job of showing but then feels compelled to add an explanation (telling). From a recent edit:

> He wrenched her from the quicksand with a last huge pull and fell back onto the ground, panting as if he'd just won a wrestling match, temporarily drained by the supreme effort.

For my money, "as if he'd just won a wrestling match, temporarily drained by the supreme effort" has already been shown by his panting and the effort he put into the rescue, so it's redundant and repetitive. I would delete it.

> He wrenched her from the quicksand with a last huge pull and fell back onto the ground, panting.

Boiled down to essentials:
- *Telling* is dispensing information.
- *Showing* is evoking experience.

With each word and phrase you write, slip into reader mode and see what the effect is: is it just informing you or bringing to life what the character experiences?

Point of view: a slippery slope

POINT OF VIEW (POV) is the perspective from which a writer tells a story. There are three basic categories. I like the way author and editor Ann Laurel Kopchik makes them clear in a post on her blog.

> All three narrative modes have a certain depth, or closeness they bring the reader to the character.
>
> *First person* (I ran from the room.) is one of the closer points of view. The reader rides along with the narrator, who is also a character in the story. That character, more or less, tells the story to the reader. Observations are filtered through the character, the reader experiences the characters thoughts, voice, and bias.
>
> *Second person* (You ran from the room.) is also one of the closer points of view, as the reader essentially becomes one of the characters in the story. Again, observations are filtered through what the reader/character experiences in the prose as well as the thoughts and voice the reader is given. However, second person can be off-putting to many readers who do not want to

be that actively or noticeably involved in a story. Some readers will have a difficult time suspending their disbelief when they read something like "You climb the stairs." Especially when they're sitting on a couch.

Third person (He/she ran from the room.) is the point of view that has various levels of reader immersion into the story and characters. An author can set the reader up as a distant observer or drop them down under the skin of one character at a time. Or the reader can end up somewhere in between those extremes. Third person is also the point of view where an author can tinker with the level of reader immersion. It does not—and probably will not—stay the same throughout the novel.

Most modern fiction is written either from the first-person or third-person point of view; second-person is seldom used. The majority is third person, and there are two basic types:

Omniscient—Like God, the narrator sees and knows everything, including all of the characters' thoughts and feelings. The narrator can and does move from one character's thoughts and experiences to another's freely. Virginia Woolf was a master of this technique. But it's a tricky one to use well, and an easy one to abuse by "head-hopping" willy-nilly from one character to another. Richard Russo, novelist, screenwriter, and lecturer at the Warren Wilson College MFA Program for Writers, wrote that using omniscience was a mature writer's technique—he didn't attempt it until he was forty.

Limited or close—The viewpoint is limited to the experiences of one character at a time—although you can tell the story from more than one character's point of view, just not all at the same time. The narrative contains nothing that a character CANNOT directly see, hear, taste, feel, think, do, or know.

In other words, just like you and me in real life. When we talk with someone, we can't know what they're thinking—unless they tell us.

When we see someone do something, we can't know their motive or purpose—unless they tell us.

If we're asleep or knocked unconscious or shot dead, the narrative from our point of view can't then show what happens to us because, well, we can't perceive it. I have seen this happen in manuscripts.

Even though I have written a novel in the first-person POV, my primary focus in this book is on close third person—for my money, it offers the most in ability to deliver the experience of a character to a reader. It has the best chance to bring the reader to being the character. And I've written four other novels that used deep third-person POV.

There are two distinct levels of limited/close third person that you can, and should, utilize.

Deep POV: Ann Laurel Kopchik makes it clear; the narrator takes on the voice of the character and the reader is deeply immersed in the character's thoughts and feelings. The reader is riding so close to the character they might be in his or her skin.

Surface POV: You can be more distant from a character's experiences at times, often at the beginning of a chapter or a scene to set the scene and orient the reader as to time, place, and what's happening. As the nature of the scene or chapter intensifies for the character, sink more deeply into their POV to deliver the experience.

The reason for using a close third person point of view is to involve your readers with your protagonist by immersing them into the character's experience. To create an emotional bond, some form of caring. If the reader cares about a character, they're a whole lot more likely to care about what happens next. And thus motivated to turn the page.

More than that, the closer you can bring a reader to a character, the tighter the emotional connection and involvement, the closer you bring a reader to experiencing the story rather than just reading information.

If that's true, then slipping out of a deep third person POV has the effect of distancing the reader from a character. Of taking her out of the mind and heart of the protagonist. Of disconnecting.

I want to show you some POV breaks that occurred in writing samples that have been sent to me. They seem innocuous, but I believe they have their effect—remember that a narrative is cumulative, and weak spots drag it down. One of my editing clients who I took to task for multiple point-of-view slips called me the "POV Nazi." You may agree with him after you read this chapter—I'm picky, picky, picky.

Subtle, small breaks in POV

Perhaps at first glance there's nothing wrong here.

> She felt radiant, and her brown eyes glistened
> with happy tears.

Here's the POV break:

> She felt radiant, and **her brown eyes glistened**
> with happy tears.

We're deep in the woman's point of view, feeling her feelings, and she can't see her eyes glisten unless she's looking into a mirror, and she's not. More than that, while she certainly knows the color of her eyes, who ever thinks about the color of their eyes when they're crying? Not me. Not anyone.

From a storytelling point of view, the reader is forced a step back from the character. Because only from *outside* the character's point of view can it be perceived that her brown eyes glisten. Okay, then how do you get images across without stepping out of her point of view? Well, in the first case you can say something such as "tears welled in her eyes." True, we don't say glistening, but the reader knows what tears in eyes look like. Basically, all the writer is trying to do here is show the reader that the character is tearing. The color of her eyes is irrelevant. Save that detail for when it actually impacts the story and affects what's happening.

I know this seems like a small thing, but the effect is cumulative. "Her brown eyes glistened" is the author's point of view, not the character's, and that pulls the reader out of the identification with the character that is so necessary for making a reader care about what happens enough to want to keep reading.

Here's another POV slip where the author intrudes. It's from within the POV of a bad guy, and the break comes with the "evil presence" reference.

> Stephenson looked down on the woman who slept unaware of the evil presence standing only yards from her tranquil slumber.

Because we're in Stephenson's point of view, he would not be standing there thinking of himself as an "evil presence." This is the author intruding to characterize him. I don't think bad guys go around thinking of themselves as evil. Sound motivation for antagonists gives them the point of view that they're doing the right or necessary thing, not something for purposes of evil.

What about this one?

> She fell to the floor, her eyes wide and panicked.

Yes, this is a subtle, tiny thing. But we're supposed to be inside her head. Where do you have to be in order to see if someone's eyes are panicked? Standing next to them, right? Unless she's standing next to herself, she can't see what her eyes look like.

The author is doing the right thing in terms of trying to use action to convey emotion, and the description does that. But it's emotion as perceived from outside the character, not inside.

Here's another little one:

> George spoke in a calm voice.

This characterization of his voice is as perceived from outside the character's mind, as heard by an objective observer. True, you can make a character aware of what his voice sounds like, e.g., "His voice sounded calm to his ears." But that's not what the author has done here.

So how can this writer get "calm voice" across without stepping out of point of view? Yes, he could listen to himself, but that wasn't the intent. It was to communicate the way the character was delivering his words. From inside the character it would be something like:

> George kept his voice calm.

POV Peeves

I have two pet peeves about point of view that I frequently see in the narratives of both unpublished and published authors:

1. Failing to maintain a steady POV
2. "Head-hopping" from one point of view to another.

I say no hops, skips, or jumps without some kind of transitional element. When you're in a POV, you should STAY in it. When I come upon POV slips, even little ones, they always pull me out of the story.

INCONSISTENT POV

Here's an example from a published novel. In a two-sentence paragraph that follows the revelation of shocking news to the character, Smith, the first sentence is this:

> Smith felt his head go light.

Other than that the writer used "felt" instead of illustrating this feeling, we're in a deep (limited) third person point of view, right inside the guy's head. Now I'll add the second sentence:

> Smith felt his head go light. Unaware of the action, he moved his free hand over his heart and clutched at his breast.

WHAM! We vault from inside the guy's head to a Godlike, omniscient POV to see action the character doesn't know is happening. For my money, any limited point of view means writing ONLY about what the character perceives, does, feels, says, etc. If he or she doesn't perceive it, it doesn't belong in that portion of the narrative. If this character is unaware of what the hand is doing, it should not be included.

One writer I know continued with the action after he had killed the point-of-view character, who could hardly be aware of what was happening around his corpse.

Worse, in the published example above, the phrase "Unaware of the action" actually refers to the lightening of the character's head in the preceding sentence rather than the hand. Ba-a-ad structure. This is from a "bestselling" author, too.

Don't you just hate it when you see published writing that's less skillful than your own?

Here's an edit that gets rid of "unaware of the action," which serves no purpose.

> Smith felt his head go light, and his hand clutched
> at his heart.

Second look: the hand part is passive and an example of a kind of filter that I call the "body parts" filter. Why not this?

> Smith felt his head go light, and he clutched at
> his heart.

Contrast the immediacy of that versus the original version:

> Smith felt his head go light. Unaware of the action, he moved his free hand over his heart and clutched at his breast.

Maintaining a solid point of view is tricky at times, and we all make these little slips, especially in a first draft when we're just trying to get the story on the page.

So keep an eye out for places where it's you, the author, seeing things and reporting on them instead of your character experiencing them from inside. The closer you keep a character's point of view, the better your chances of involving your reader more and more deeply.

Head-hopping

WHEN YOU USE an omniscient (third-person) point of view, it is appropriate to skillfully move from one character's point of view to another's. The omniscient approach, used well, doesn't seek to imitate the close third person technique. The trouble comes when a writer uses the deep third person POV from character to character to character while shifting from inside one head to inside another at will within a scene and with no transition.

Here's an example from the published novel we just looked at. At this point, the author has been using Smith's deep third person point of view for several pages. The paragraph below is tightly inside Smith's point of view, in his head.

> Smith knew that this meant the suspect would probably wind up going to the hospital. The idea didn't much appeal to him. "Get him in a cell."

So far, so good. Now for the following paragraph.

> Jones shrugged. It wasn't that he cared, but Smith's suggestion ran counter to protocol. He wanted to cover himself. "Clear him here first, then."

Whoa. We went from knowing what Smith knows and feels about an idea directly into what Jones feels and desires. Mental whiplash for this reader. Again, this blatant head-hopping occurred after many pages that had held tightly to Smith's point of view. For me, this is sloppy, undisciplined writing (or editing). As it happens, Jones was a minor character who disappeared in a sentence or two anyway, so I have to wonder why the author felt the need to include what he felt and wanted. I'd cut all but the dialogue and maybe suggest some visualization of Jones's discomfort from Smith's point of view—but no interior monologue.

What's the harm in this? I believe that, at some level, head-hopping reduces/damages/breaks the emotional bond the writer has worked so hard to create by being in the close third person. Why? Because the hand of the author is clearly revealed and the reader, either consciously or somewhere down under, feels the manipulation of an external force, which is contrary to being carried along with what's happening to the character she's involved with. The emotional effect of the narrative is diminished and, as Sol Stein says, creating emotion in a reader is the author's job.

You see plenty of head-hopping in published works, and I wondered if I was taking the wrong stance in being so critical of it. So I surveyed a number of New York publishing pros—editors and agents—for their views. Here are some of the responses:

AN EXECUTIVE EDITOR'S VIEW OF HEAD-HOPPING

I share your peeve about "head-hopping"— apt term. So thanks for letting me blather on about it.

I think it's OK to do it so long as there is only one point of view per *discernible section.* *(RR: emphasis mine.)* That is to say, so long as there's something to represent to the reader that there has been some kind of jump. A chapter or a space break or something.

But when it happens in the middle of continuous action, it's a serious problem. Basically, if you tell your story with recourse to everyone's head at all times, you're throwing out all the rules and permitting yourself everything. And if you are permitting yourself everything, then you also forfeit the right to hide anything of narrative importance—who the killer is, for instance—without cheating in a major way.

I've always tried to tell the writers I work with that some kind of consistency of point of view—some ground rules that the reader can grasp—is an essential element of what is an epistemological problem. How does the reader know what he knows? Of course the author knows everything in advance—after all, he came up with the story. But he has to maintain the illusion that the reader and the narrative are on the same footing, discovering at the same time what the author has cooked up. After all, once the reader knows everything, the narrative is over.

Mystery stories are great examples of this kind of narrative epistemology. I always pointed out to the writers I worked with that all the Sherlock Holmes tales were narrated in the first person and by Holmes's friend, for very sound reasons. Had Doyle used third person, a reader might well ask, "If you are employing the omniscient narrator, then you know everything, including the killer's identity. In which case you should tell us!" Whereas by using Dr. Watson, he shields himself from this accusation. Dr. Watson can't possibly know the outcome in advance, and so he reports on the action and shares with the reader the process of discovery. Watson knows enough to introduce Holmes to the reader, but once the story starts, he knows as much as the reader does.

With the advent in the twentieth century of close third person, the objection on the basis of omniscience is less relevant. A writer can use a kind of limited omniscience narrative. And I think that's OK. Provided nothing is hidden. Agatha Christie used to use a Dr. Watson-like device for her Poirot novels, but then got rid of it, no doubt when she realized that simply following Poirot in close(-enough) third person was sufficient.

Still, that doesn't excuse her gross violation of this principle in *The ABC Murders,* where she expands her omniscience but nonetheless hides crucial elements from the reader merely as a ploy to keep the mystery going.

So I think it's very important, in head-hopping, to keep the points of view distinct through the use of clearly demarked boundaries—space breaks, chapters, etc.—and also to make sure that each point of view is seen divulging the entirety of its knowledge of the narrative.

(RR: Rather than "head-hopping," I think of this approach as "point-of-view shifts." The former involves sudden, unrestricted, unmotivated jumps in the midst of action while the latter uses clearly

signaled breaks limited to reasonably long, discreet segments of narrative.)

Nonetheless, I do see many bestselling works of fiction that practice 'head-hopping' in continuous action, and no one seems to care. Well, not 'no one,' but nearly—I thought I was it until your email came along.

Perhaps in terms of encouraging writers, it's best to focus on what consistency in use of point of view can deliver, and get away from what it's meant to avoid. The masterpieces of unreliable narration, from *The Aspern Papers* to *The Remains of the Day*—not to mention Ron Howard's adaptation of *A Beautiful Mind*—all attest to the power of point of view. In other words, don't make point of view just a vehicle of narrative, make it a partner, or a driving force, in narrative.

I've a client who, when I pointed out how much she hopped from head to head, told me that head-hopping was common in her romance sub-genre. Yet I know an editor with a firm that publishes a lot of romance who hates hates hates head-hopping—and summarily rejects novels that do it.

A top New York literary agent wrote to say

I am in absolute agreement with you. People do it, but, for the most part, it doesn't work (I'm not going to say never, because this is fiction we're talking about, not algebra). "Hopping," as you've put it, distances the reader from the close emotional connection with the central point-of-view character in the scene, it draws attention to the fact that writing is an artifice (destroying the "suspension of disbelief" that reading a novel usually though not always entails), and it generally just plain sounds awkward. Unless it's masterfully pulled off, it usually signals a lack of control of authorial voice, to my mind.

ANOTHER EDITOR'S VIEW

An editor at a major New York imprint opined,

> I am not overly troubled by rotating POV if the writer can sustain the variety of voices and allow the reader to maintain clarity in his/her mind about who is whom. Singular POV is not sacrosanct, in my opinion.

Here, though, because he uses the term "rotating," I think the editor is actually talking about skillful use of multiple points of view, not bolting from head to head within a scene. Saying "maintain clarity" is also a clue to what he means.

As with just about anything in writing long-form fiction or memoir, there aren't really any rules. But I don't think there's an agent or editor who has a problem with a consistent, "non-hoppy" narrative, so why take the chance of (a) running into someone who hates it, and (b) distancing your reader from your characters?

Here's something on the subject I found on English teacher and author Crawford Kilian's the *Fiction Writer's Page* website that describes "episodically limited third-person omniscient POV," a single close third-person narrator. He also describes using the POV character's voice as the narrator when in deep third person as I suggest for characterizing each character's narrative.

> Whoever is the point of view for a particular scene determines the persona. An archbishop

sees and describes events from his particular point of view, while a pickpocket does so quite differently. So the narrator, in a scene from the archbishop's point of view, has a persona quite different from that of the pickpocket: a different vocabulary, a different set of values, a different set of priorities. As a general rule, *point of view should not change **during** a scene. (emphasis mine)* So if an archbishop is the point of view in a scene involving him and a pickpocket, we shouldn't suddenly switch to the pickpocket's point of view until we've resolved the scene and moved on to another scene.

You can change POV within scenes if you clearly differentiate and integrate them. In a fast-action scene involving characters the reader knew well, I used the following technique to create a whole with their separate parts by using a break with ellipses to signal a change in point of view yet keep the action moving smoothly:

> Marion screamed. The woman turned toward her and shot.
> The bullet slammed into Marion's neck—
>
> • • •
>
> Karl watched Marion fall. It seemed like slow motion. This couldn't be real. He ran down the aisle toward her.

Story as garden

WHILE ENJOYING ONE of my favorite films, *The Abyss*, I was reminded of the need for effective "seeding" of character and action. The film does it well.

At one point a roughneck in the crew holds up his massive fist and tells a buddy that "they used to call this the hammer." That nicely sets up a time later in the film when he knocks a bad guy head over keister with one mighty punch. Because of the setup, it was absolutely credible. (Well, the guy's size was a part of that, too.)

Another fine setup had to do with the hero's wedding ring as a life-saving device. After a spat between Bud and Lindsey, his about-to-be-divorced wife (and the heroine), he throws his wedding band in a toilet. He leaves. Comes back and fishes the ring out. Cut to extreme close-up of wedding band going back on his finger.

While at the time this seemed pointed at characterizing him and his feelings about her—and it did that—it turned out that wasn't everything it did. They're on the ocean floor, and later in the film the hold he is in is flooding. He dashes for an already-closing hatch door and manages to put a hand into the gap. Ordinarily his hand would have been crushed by the hydraulic door, but it's not. Yep, his wedding ring stops the door from closing all the way.

Rescuers come and the door is opened. But that must have been one helluva wedding ring.

Without the setup, the ring-stopping-the-door trick would have been a mini *deus ex machina* and a laughable coincidence. These "seedlings" in the film work so well because they don't call attention to themselves when they happen and just seem like normal parts of what's happening. Thank you, excellent screenwriter, for your good gardening.

A mystery writer must, of course, plant clues—interesting how even the language for doing this kind of thing is from gardening—but the rest of us need to pay attention to our seeding as well for motivating both action and characterization.

In a romance novel I recently edited, almost at the end of the book the heroine is groped from behind in a public place by a man whom she assumes to be her current love. She goes along with it because they've made love in risky places before. Unfortunately, it's her old lover doing the groping. As bad luck would have it, her current guy bursts in on the scene. Despite her sincere explanations, he goes into a jealous snit and declares that the relationship won't work. Goodbye.

All good grist for the romance mill . . . but for one thing. The current guy has been Mister Adoring Puppy the whole way. He has accepted her dalliance with a celebrity in the beginning of the relationship, including a hot sleepover. He has been accommodating in every way, constantly declaring his love with words and actions. That's another thing I talked to the writer about—the guy is just too perfect. No flaws. No character arc. No contention between him and her except for the beforementioned snit.

The problem with how he reacted to this incident was that the motivation for a strong jealous reaction had never been set up. To react strongly was out of character for this character. Luckily, it didn't have to be, and I was able to suggest to the writer how to fix it by drawing on other material already in the story. It seems that the protagonist's first love was jealous and, whenever she even spoke to another man, he would put his arm around her and interfere. If the writer has Mr. Perfect do something similar (an action to which she can react, thereby inserting even more characterization for her) and exhibit a bit of jealousy, then his motive for the later scene will be established and it will be credible.

"POST-SEEDING"

Computers are wonderful in the way they give you the ability to go back and change things in the earlier pages of a novel quickly and easily when a late thought creates the need for seeding a development in your story. Here's an example of "post-seeding."

About a third of the way into a novel, the female protagonist needs to be pulled out of a suicidal dive caused by the tragic death of her once-in-a-lifetime love. She encounters a small boy who seems to suffer from autism. She is a healer and is sympathetic, but his condition and innocence didn't seem like motive enough to stir her from her depression.

So what would? How about if the child reminded her in a specific, powerful way of the man she had loved and lost? So the author went back to the scene leading to her love's death and gave him a "little-boy-lost" look that had always melted her heart. Then the narrative showed her seeing that same look in the eyes of the boy. That stimulus started her on the path of helping the child, which ultimately brought her back to emotional life.

The phrase "little-boy-lost" was seeded in three places that added up to strong, clear motivation for her when the right time came. By the way, the seed had to be distinctive enough to be easily recalled when it affected the story; in this case, "little-boy-lost" not only fit unobtrusively the first time it was used, i.e., didn't call attention to itself, it was distinct enough to remember later.

In the example from *The Abyss*, it was an extreme close-up of Bud putting the ring back on that made it memorable when, in another extreme close-up, his hand was in the door.

So seed your novel with small things early on that grow to be significant. And don't hesitate to go back and plow up early ground to plant the antecedents of characters and events that come into being in the process of discovering your story.

Linger for involving storytelling

I TOOK A COURSE IN literary manuscript development at the University of Washington from novelist Laura Kalpakian. She gave my storytelling high marks for dialogue, description, and pace—but she didn't get enough from my narrative about the characters to truly involve her, to make her care. For her, my narrative was simply too lean at times for her to experience what was happening to the character in a way that connected with her.

Her wise advice: "Linger."

The following paragraph comes from a writer's sample that I critiqued in my blog. In the scene, a teenage boy is approaching a girl's home for his first date with her, and he's never been there.

> Her mother opened the door as he approached. "Come right in. Kathy isn't ready yet; it'll be just a minute." He found himself in the living room with her mother, father, and little brother. He tried not to say much, passing the time, trying to get through the ordeal without coming apart.

In this writer's haste to get the boy and girl out the door and to their date, he's missed opportunities to draw the reader into the boy's story and build sympathy for his character, not to mention create tension and story questions about what's going to happen. Anybody who's been a teenage boy calling on a girl for the first time knows how tense the situation and the boy are. The narrative would be far better served with a brief scene instead of the summary done here. For example, just one of the rich possibilities to explore in a scene is the look the father gives the boy (for he would give him a look, I'm certain), and the boy's perception/reaction to it.

> Kathy's father lowered his bushy brows and gave Jimmy a look that made him feel like he was lying under an X-ray machine. He jerked a quick little smile and blurted, "Pleased to meet you, sir." Then he realized how stupid that was because nobody had actually introduced them. The sweat under his arms cranked up to a steady drip.

I would linger more in that living room to capture character and build tension. In this writer's manuscript, all too quickly he had the teenagers escape the girl's house and go to a dance in the high school gym. When they dance close, she gives signals of interest such as pressing tightly against him, and he becomes aroused. When they leave the dance, the writer gives us this:

> At twelve, he guided Kathy to their coats and out into the frosty October air. The car heater kicked in nicely as they drove down Main Street and into the countryside. The farms they passed were dark. Jamie turned down a gravel road and slowed.

The night is frosty, but what else is there when they walk out of that gym? There's no tension or anticipation in this expository paragraph, but great opportunity to build it. Is there a moon out? Mightn't he gaze at her face and have some romantic/lusty thoughts as he takes her to the car? If it's like any high school dance I ever went to back in the day, there are kids outside, some smoking, some necking. For example, what if we lingered just a bit like this?

> At midnight, he guided Kathy to their coats and out into the frosty October air. Laughter and the sweet aroma of cigarette smoke wafted from three guys huddled beside a pickup truck. When Jimmy and Kathy passed a parked car with steamed-up windows, he heard thumping and the car rocked on its springs. He glanced at Kathy and found her gazing at the car. If only . . .
>
> She looked up at him and grinned. She tip-toed and leaned against him to whisper into his ear, pressing her belly against his hand. "I don't have to be home until one."
>
> Oh, man . . .

That little bit of description and action didn't take many words, but you get a greater sense of place and time, and the sexual tension between the two is ramped up. As a result, the coming necking and petting when they park will be that much more meaningful.

Stay with scenes long enough to enrich them with "story meaning"—character emotions and reactions to settings and happenings that deepen the reader's understanding and connection.

Lingering means to take the time to let your characters come to life on the page with action that characterizes them and advances the story.

From there to here, then to now

OFTEN IN AN EDIT I'll see a need for a transition when writers sometimes just leap over time and space without giving the reader a clue as to what's going on. This is caused, I suspect, by the usual syndrome—the writer sees all in his/her head but just doesn't get it on the page.

So how do you get from there to here... or from then to now? I advocate using character and action. The following example is a simple shift from one location to another; such a transition, in a book, would include a blank line between paragraphs like this to denote a change in place or time.

> Jennifer knew there was only one place to find Jason. She raced out the door and down the stairs to the parking garage.

> As soon as she hit the smoky air in Timothy's Tavern it hit right back—eyes, throat, lungs. God, how could Jason stand this?

What the reader knows without being shown:
- Jennifer drove to the tavern (she raced to her parking garage).

- She has parked her car and come in (she is inside the tavern).

Note how the transition is motivated by action that leads the reader to expect movement. In the second part, the transition lets you know immediately that we're in a different place, Timothy's Tavern, and not the garage.

What is not needed because it has no impact on the story:

- Getting Jennifer into her car.
- Showing Jennifer driving down Main Street and taking a hard left on Pine.
- Slamming the door of her car and racing across the parking lot at Timothy's Tavern.
- Opening the door to Timothy's Tavern and running in.

Here's an example from my edit files of a narrative that needs transitional work. It's from a paranormal vampire romance. I'll give it to you straight, then with the comments I gave the author.

> She slowed her breathing and reached for the deep sleep. Instinctively, her mind connected with Randall's. Together, they drifted into sleep. Their breath left their bodies at the same time. Their hearts stopped beating as one.
>
> Randall stared at the faces gathered before him. Some of them were good friends, others were mortal enemies. He took a deep breath and said firmly, "I've called this Council today to introduce my intention to take a mate."

They're asleep and then suddenly Randall is staring into faces. It's not my job, as an editor, to create a transition for an author—but it is my job to point out the need and make suggestions.

Here, along with a little line editing and comments (italicized), is what I did:

She slowed her breathing and reached for the deep sleep. Instinctively, her mind connected with Randall's. Together, they drifted into sleep. Their breath left their bodies at the same time. Their hearts stopped beating as one.

* * *

(I added a line space and asterisks to indicate changes in point of view and scene.)
Randall stared at the faces gathered before him. *(A little transition and scene-setting would be good. Even "That night," would help. What time of the day/night is it? Where are they? How many council members? What are the attitudes emanating from them? Is Randall on his throne? "Faces" suggests a clump of people standing before him? Are they? Or are they sitting in chairs? Around a table? What?)* Some were good friends, others mortal enemies. *(Technically, "faces" can't be friends or enemies. How about: Some of them belonged to good friends, others to mortal enemies.)* He took a deep breath and said firmly, "I've called this Council today to introduce my intention to take a mate."

There are times an author, lost in the fullness of her understanding of the story, shortchanges the reader on the transition from time to time, place to place, or person to person. I'm sure you've had the disorienting experience of sailing along in a narrative only to suddenly become lost when the storyteller vaults to an unexpected somewhere/somewhen/someone else.

Transitions can—and often should—be simple and virtually unnoticeable. At other times, they are a valuable tool for enriching the story by characterizing through description or action.

Following are examples of four transitional techniques using examples gleaned from manuscripts.

FROM HERE TO THERE

We start with the character in her bedroom:

> I lie back down, but there's no chance of me going back to sleep now, so I get up and put the kettle on. As I sit down with a cup of tea, Amy appears.

I was okay with this through putting the kettle on, but then where does she sit down? In her room? In the kitchen? If it's in the kitchen, the writer needs to locate her there for the reader. Perhaps dress her—when she rises, does she put on a robe or clothes? Are sounds of other people in the flat, is anyone is in the kitchen or it is blessedly empty, etc. Let us see her in action.

Another "here to there" slip with vampires in a bedroom:

> With no more than a thought, he dressed them both for the banquet. Alex looked down at the beautiful crimson gown and reached up to feel her intricately done hair. Damien's power was so easy to him, so effortless. It was one more difference between the two of them.
>
> Alex said, "I'm going back to my old room, Damien."
>
> "You will not," Damien said, his voice steely. "You will cease this foolishness right now. You forget who is master here." He grabbed her arm.
>
> He was interrupted by a vampyress who came sailing out of the banquet to catch his arm.

In this case, the author was so eager to get to the coming conflict at the banquet she forgot to transport us there. The fix could be as simple as adding a line break after the first paragraph—before Alex's dialogue—and a snippet of transition:

> . . . It was one more difference between the two of them.
>
> Just outside the banquet room, Alex said, "I'm going back to my old room . . ."

FROM TIME TO TIME

In another novel, we're at a cockfight and the roosters have been set loose:

> They danced at first, happy to be on their feet as if they'd kiss, but then something within them said "KILL" and they lunged like Spartans with green head feathers, short-handled daggers and form-fitting breast plates. Oooh's and ahh's followed every thrust and bend. Feathers floated away from wounds like wishes from dandelions. Screams and battle-cry cackles sounded out pain and laughter.
>
> The sight of the loser went right through me. A beaten soldier on the battlefield after the last bayonet strike. Lying limp and shaking, pecked to near death, eyes out, broken wings, wounds gaping.

If the writer is going to jump to the end of the fight, we need a time transition. First, an extra line space between the paragraphs is a customary—and useful—way to indicate a gap in time. In manuscript form, adding a centered "#" helps clue in the reader, though it may not be needed in printed form.

In this case, I don't even know how long one of these matches lasts. Minutes? An hour? A transition and some information would be good. For instance, after a blank line break, add . . .

> "*Twenty bloody minutes later,* the sight of the loser went right through me."

FROM PERSON TO PERSON

Transitions between characters can be simple or complex. The following example moves from one character to another within a chapter, but carefully—in my view, head-hopping should be avoided at all costs.

This transition uses a line break with centered asterisks to signal shifting from one POV to another. But it takes more to make the shift seamless and effortless. Here, the action of one character is tied to the other so the scene seems to flow continuously even though there is a point-of-view shift.

> She mounted the steps and came upon a slender man in a black overcoat. The man aimed a small video camera her way. As she turned her face away, she saw his lips move, and the wind carried his words to her.
>
> He said, "I think I got one."
>
> She looked behind her. Nothing of interest there. Shielding her face with her scarf, she shifted her gaze to the man, and he jerked the camera away. He wanted to conceal his purpose.
>
> But what did it matter? It could have nothing to do with her.
>
> * * *

"I think I got one." The whisper shivered in KB Volmer's earpiece. She stepped out of the gallery of art done by kids in Ireland. It hadn't looked any better than the stuff her mother had taped on the refrigerator when she was a kid. Speaking just loudly enough for her collar mike to pick up her words, she said, "Again."

"I got one."

Tying two characters' actions together in this way also works when moving from the end of a chapter to the beginning of the next.

THE JUMP-CUT TRANSITION

Sometimes no transition at all is the way to go if you can use jump cuts to collapse time for powerful pacing.

In film, "jump cuts" are often used to collapse time. The moniker is literal—in the midst of a scene the action jumps ahead from one moment to one further down the timeline rather than following all of the action as it happens. The technique accelerates pace and can enhance the impact of the action.

Jump cuts work in fiction, too, but care has to be taken with setting the scene. In a film, the viewer sees a complete picture at all times. In fiction, we have to supply it with words. And that's where I see writers missing the mark.

Chapters are a great opportunity for using jump cuts. You can end a chapter or scene in one place, wrapping up an action and setting up a future course, and then jump to a completely different scene . . . as long as you fill the reader in on what that new scene is.

Here's an example. In my novel, *Hiding Magic (2015),* Annie is arrested by Homeland Security and an agent uses torture that could take her life. The action takes place in Chicago in the midst of winter, and the reader has been freezing along with Annie in this chapter. She escapes her holding cell and the chapter ends this way:

> She dashed to the doorway marked Exit and hurtled down the stairs.

We next see the character in the Florida Everglades. In real time, she would need to leave the building, go to O'Hare Airport, buy a ticket, get on a plane, land elsewhere, rent a vehicle, and travel. Ho hum. Instead, here's the jump cut to the opening of the next chapter:

> Eager to see the ships of her clan, Annie peered ahead as she steered an airboat through saw-grass marsh deep within the three million acres of the Everglades.
>
> The warm air coddled her, such a relief from the energy drain of keeping warm in Chicago. Sunset colored the sky with bands of pink and mauve. A silhouetted heron winged past, grace in motion. After traveling all night and most of the day, she relished the idea of coming to rest.

The first sentence, a mere twenty-eight words, quickly transports the character to a place a thousand miles away. Note that it does so from within her point of view, giving the reader a sense of character through her reactions to where she is and at the same time enabling the reader to "see" the character's surroundings.

Hiding Magic's other primary protagonist, Gabe, was also captured and tortured by the agent. He was broken out from his cell by Drago. Gabe and Annie are destined to travel very different paths before they are reunited.

Here's Gabe's escape scene.

> Drago opened a door to a stairwell. "Quickly, others may come."
>
> Gabe followed him up toward the roof. What did Drago have up there, a helicopter? A magic broom? It didn't matter to Gabe, anything to get away from people determined to torture and kill him.

So they go into the night. The story calls for Gabe to go with Drago to his home place, which would involve climbing the stairs, getting onto the vehicle Drago has on the roof, and traveling across Chicagoland in the dark to a forest preserve. But that's not action that will move the plot along. So, at the beginning of Gabe's new chapter, we jump:

> A moan broke Gabe free from a nightmare and he bolted upright. It had been his voice, a teeth-clenched cry forced out by a vision of himself frozen upright, white with frost, arms reaching for his son but doomed to never embrace him.
>
> A quilt fell from him and cold air struck his bare torso. The bed was a bunk fastened to a paneled wall. The room wasn't much more than sleeping quarters, maybe six feet by eight. There was space enough in a corner for an antique-looking washstand and an old-fashioned pitcher in a large bowl. Neatly folded, a small towel and washcloth waited next to it.
>
> His shirt and jeans were draped over a single chair. Reddish sunlight glowed through

a porthole.
    A porthole?

We're off and running in a new place that is clearly very strange to Gabe as we experience it from within his point of view.

When you jump cut, make sure you give the reader solid footing when he lands so that he knows where he is. Do it from within the character's experience so description becomes part of the action, not simple exposition.

Flashing back

FLASHBACKS ARE RISKY. You chance losing readers (like me) who really, really, really want to know what's going to happen next which, if you've done your job, is exactly what they should be interested in. You've worked hard to immerse them in the NOW of the story and they don't want to be yanked out to go to THEN.

When should you use flashbacks, if at all? Editors and agents see scores of manuscripts with openings slowed to a halt by the weight of flashbacks and explanatory exposition.

Some say to never use them, and that's possible. But there are times a flashback can enrich a story, adding depth and meaning that would otherwise not be there. There are times when, without knowledge of the past, a character's actions will seem unmotivated, and thus not credible.

So when and how do you use flashbacks? I advocate using them only when the knowledge revealed in the flashback is *absolutely critical* for understanding what's going on in the story's present. Beginning writers need to be tough on themselves here. They'll feel like a reader needs to know things about a character that, truthfully, are not necessary for understanding the NOW of the story. It's the NOW that readers want to be immersed in.

Another reason for flashbacks is necessary characterization—an example is coming right up.

We pause for notes on how to create a flashback that works.

> Weave it as seamlessly as possible into the action. Words such as "remembered" and phrases such as "thought of the time when" are bright red flags that signal to readers that coming soon to a page near them is a part to skip. Transitions are key.
>
> Make the flashback a true scene with action, dialogue, tension, and all the storytelling elements that you use to keep a reader engaged. Avoid telling a past event, show it (unless it can be done in one brief, crisp paragraph). Readers want to experience what's happening, not just receive information. A good flashback, for the moment, becomes the "now" of the story.

Here's an example from *Hiding Magic* of slipping from the present to the past and back in order to give the reader necessary information about a character. Note: *lledri* refers to energy these people can manipulate like magic, *lessi* is ordinary people. The scene is in present tense and then simply shifts to past tense for the flashback.

> I shiver. Without Graeme, I have no more life to live.
>
> He was so full of life the day we strolled through Central Park . . . if only I hadn't said that I thought the Met's new sculpture exhibit was excellent.
>
> Graeme shrugged. "Perhaps." He gestured at the people who plodded through the park. "But there's little else of excellence from that sorry race."

My contrary side reared its head at the unfairness of the bias against the *lessi* that Graeme inherited from his father. "There's plenty of good in them, and you know it."

"I do not." He surveyed the people around us. Dozens wandered, for it was a sunny day. "Observe their colors, Annie. Is there kindness or good will anywhere?"

I looked, and the *lledri* auras around their heads writhed with the nasty burgundy of hostility, the bilious color of lies, the ash-violet of depression, and the bruised red of violence. That, of course, only served to rally my resistance. "Perhaps not here, not now, but there are many good-hearted *lessi*."

He made an exaggerated moue and said, "A wager?"

I picked up the gauntlet. "Yes." I pointed down a curving walk. "We'll go that way, and we'll find a worthy *lessi*."

"The stakes?"

I ran my hands over my breasts and down my belly.

Oh, that smile of his. He said, "It's a bet."

Only minutes later I congratulated herself on my good luck when we came upon a woman pulling a two-wheeled shopping cart; her aura radiated a rosy gold, the rich hue of caring. Perhaps sixty years old, the woman was stout, anchored to the earth like an oak tree. She stopped before a trio of homeless men who sprawled on ragged blankets.

When she opened a brown paper bag from

her cart, I caught the aroma of bologna. The woman took a sandwich from the sack and handed it to one of the men. He sat up and attacked the food.

Graeme spread his arms in surrender, lifted his gaze to the heavens and said, as if to a higher power, "Why have you once again given Annie victory over your poor servant Graeme?"

I poked him in his ribs. "I believe you owe me."

He pulled me into his arms and pressed me to him. "I'm ready."

His body let me know that he was indeed ready. My pulse quickened, and I wanted to take him by the hand, find a cluster of bushes, cast a shadow illusion for concealment, and make love. But I pushed away and said, "If we're so advanced, we should help."

Oh, if only I hadn't . . .

He laughed, and then put on a thick French accent. "But of course, *ma cherie*." Stepping to the woman's side, he gestured to the sack of sandwiches and said, "May I?"

She smiled and nodded, and Graeme took a sandwich from the bag and thrust it at a whiskery man whose bristles made him look like a wild boar.

The boar man scrambled to his feet, digging into a pocket. Too late I *saw* in his aura the acrid tornado of colors that meant madness. He pulled a knife from a pocket, flicked it open and thrust it into Graeme's chest. Graeme collapsed as if he were a puppet whose strings had been cut.

I dropped to my knees beside him and

> plunged *lledri* into his chest to heal the wound—
> but his heart had been sliced almost in two. There
> was no way I could mend him in time. I looked
> into his eyes and saw terrible fear . . . and then
> an even more terrible absence.
> If only I hadn't . . . if only . . .

The use of "if only I hadn't" bookends to begin and end the flashback eases you into the past and then back to the present. Connective tissue such as this can help move your reader into and out of a flashback and help tie its meaning to the story.

This example, brief as it is (just two manuscript pages), expands the reader's understanding of why the character is depressed and suicidal, yet it has conflict and tension.

Later, to deepen the reader's understanding of the other primary protagonist, the novel uses a mini-flashback to plant the seed for a longer one that adds to characterization later. First, the mini-flash using the *telling* mode rather than *showing:*

> Gabe has never found a word for what he sees
> when people lie. Aura? But it isn't a glow so much
> as streaming sparks of translucent, luminescent
> color. He's never heard of anyone else seeing
> them. People would probably think it was a good
> thing, being able to tell when people lie. But he
> hates it. He's felt *outside* since he was seven and
> perceiving the color of a lie in action cost him
> his best friend.

The character's feeling of not belonging is a powerful motivator for later action, and this glimpse will need expanding—but not at this time in the story. The full history wasn't needed for understanding the scene, but his ability to use *lledri* needed to be introduced, along with planting the seed for a flashback that later expands the experience that motivates his feelings.

His son has inherited his ability, and the effect on the boy resembles autism, which is something the father needs to understand. So, eighty-five pages later, when the other protagonist says to him "You know the effect that possessing this ability can have on a child, don't you?" this is Gabe's response:

> Oh, yeah, Gabe knows how seeing a weird color in the air can affect a kid. In second grade, he'd seen Marty Simmons swipe an oatmeal cookie from Heather's lunch sack. It was scorched on the bottom like all the cookies Heather's mom made. When Heather saw Marty eating it, she accused him of taking her cookie.
>
> He told her his mom had baked cookies yesterday and that Heather was crazy—and a nasty greenish color had flickered around his head. Gabe studied the other kids at the table as they watched Marty tell his lie. Their eyes never shifted and they never reacted to the color swirling around Marty's head, not even when Heather started to cry.
>
> They just couldn't see it. Gabe had decided he wasn't crazy because he knew what he saw was true, but he felt . . . *outside*, as though he was across the room from everybody else. Gabe had wanted to ask his mother about it, but he'd been afraid she would look at him in that scared-angry way that said he was nuts . . . strange . . . weird.
>
> Soon he'd had no friends, and it wasn't until his mother moved and he changed schools that

he was able to make himself pretend he was like everybody else and be friendly again.

Both the "mini flash" and the longer flashback were tied directly to the action in the scenes, and the longer one briefly summarizes a scene complete with action and conflict.

Still, my advice is to keep flashbacks to a minimum and for sure to avoid launching into one within the first few pages of your story.

Description Techniques

Without description, a novel would be no different than a print-out of a radio commercial. We're all familiar with the primary purpose of description:

> To show a place or illustrate action

But when you write for effect, description doesn't stop there. As you'll see, description is capable of this:

> Adding to characterization

That's the plus side. There are hazards to avoid in description, too:

- Filters that distance readers
- Conclusion words
- Goofy staging of action
- Overwriting

First up: experiential description, a key tool for characterization.

Make it experiential to characterize

THE READER OF A NOVEL or a memoir wants the narrative to create a very specific effect: he wants to be taken away from the real world he sits in. He wants to feel and see and do things he would never do. Readers want to experience the world of the novel. To be immersed in it so that the real world ceases to exist.

That's your task: to create an experience. It is not to tell a story. It is to cause a specific reaction in your reader's mind. A suspension of disbelief, a connection *to the life of a character.* Characters are the key to and core of creating an experience for the reader.

The cartoon above shows an experience, and you can see it. In a story, you can describe the action with words. Simply describing it can't give you the character's full experience, but there's a way to characterize through description to deliver it.

This relates to the old saw, "show, don't tell." Telling is the mere delivery of information. A newspaper does that. A novel or memoir should be delivering a character's experience.

Description is a key element of every novel, every scene. Where a scene happens needs to be set (described) so the reader has a context within which to experience what the character experiences. Description is needed to show action, of course. In a novel, descriptions shouldn't be simple photographs of what the character sees. Oh, they can be and often are, but snapshots don't create an experience. They are telling, they are information, they are not emotion, they are not experience.

The best description happens from within the character's point of view, colored by the character's emotions, needs, beliefs, and desires.

It characterizes.

DESCRIBE FROM THE INSIDE, NOT THE OUTSIDE

Here's description from a writer's sample where characterization could have happened but didn't. The writer describes Jimmy and his girlfriend this way:

> Jimmy was high-school skinny, that lean, still-growing time when muscles are tight everywhere and the sinews are loose and respond quickly. He wasn't tall, only five seven, but she was only five three and they appeared to be the perfect couple.

I liked "high-school skinny," but these lines are clearly the author getting some exposition out of the way—we're taken out of the boy's head and made to feel distant from the scene. The phrase "they appeared to be the perfect couple" is clearly from another point of view entirely since the boy can't see what they look like together. Not to mention a first-degree case of telling.

I know it's tough to describe a character when you're in his point of view, and you don't want to resort to the tired old idea of looking in a mirror, but there are ways to do it. For example:

> Jimmy worried Kathy would think he was too skinny, which his mother said was just because he was still growing, all sinewy with long lean muscles. But he wasn't so worried about being

only five foot seven—Kathy was maybe five three,
tops, and he thought they made a perfect couple.

As you can see, this gives a picture of them but characterizes
him as well, and it comes from inside the character, not from
outside, from the author. The reader not only doesn't leave the
character's head, she is drawn more deeply into it.

EXPERIENTIAL DESCRIPTION OF PLACE

Well done description can enable a reader to "be" there. In my
view, that falls short of the goal. With experiential description,
you can enable the reader to be *the character* there.

When you "see" a place through a character's point of view,
you can do two things at once: set the scene to give the reader the
context in which things are happening and show a character's
personality.

Here's an example: a mailroom in a large corporation seen as
a simple snapshot, the approach many writers take to description.

In a gray room with fluorescent lights, a rack of
pigeonholes for sorting mail sat along one wall.
Next to them stood a wheeled delivery cart, a desk
with a computer on it, and a worn swivel chair.

Now let's describe that same setting in a way that characterizes
a middle-aged man who works in the mailroom. Every element
from the snapshot above is included, but they are used as ways
to characterize.

Jeff switched on the mailroom lights. The
fluorescents glared at him the way they had for
fifteen years, and the gray walls radiated depression. The rack of pigeonholes along one wall for

sorting mail stared at him, each empty hole like his life. The delivery cart stood ready to cause the daily pain in his hip when he trudged through the offices, delivering mail to people who didn't see him, like he was furniture.

On his desk the computer waited to be turned on—no, they said "booted up," didn't they—its programs lurking, waiting to trip him up again when he tried to send out a shipment. He sat in his beat-up swivel chair, and a small sense of comfort came with the way the worn cushions conformed to his body and it squeaked when he tilted back.

Just as the snapshot approach did, this experiential description gave you a picture of the room and what was in it, so it served the purpose of setting the scene. But it also defined Jeff's character.

The same room described through another character's point of view has the same physical characteristics but can be a very different place. Here's the room described through the point of view of Jinny, a twenty-something new employee.

Jinny burst through the mailroom door and was disappointed yet again to see Jeff already there. One of these days she'd beat him in and do the setup. He hadn't even turned on the computer yet. She reached past him, slumped as usual in that crummy old swivel chair with the ratty cushion—why didn't he requisition something decent?—and flicked on the computer. When break came and he went out for a smoke she'd surf her favorite blogs.

The gray walls under the soft fluorescent light

> soothed her headache. The racks of pigeonholes
> waited for her to fill their mouths with the mail
> that helped the company function. The delivery
> cart stood ready—maybe today she'd ask Jeff if
> she could be the one that wheeled it through the
> cubicles, saying hi, meeting people. Even though
> she'd only been here a month, the mailroom felt
> like an old friend.

Same pigeonholes, same everything picture-wise, but very different characterization—that's experiential description.

Whenever we are in a place, we not only see what's in it, we react to what's there in ways that characterize us. Have your characters do the same, and color their perceptions with the result.

When we drive up to the place we live, we don't just see a building. We might see a warm home where we live lovingly with our family—or we might see the place where a cruel stepfather tortures us every day. You can bet your perceptions of that building will be different depending on which of those places it is for you.

EXPERIENTIAL DESCRIPTION OF ACTION

Experiential description means that the exact same action, as experienced by two different characters, is a very different experience for each character and, thus, for the reader.

First, the scene as if it were viewed through an objective camera:

> Morticia leaned forward and her nostrils flared.
> She sank her fangs into Frank's neck. Blood rushed
> into her mouth and dribbled down his neck. He
> moaned and writhed, but she pinned him to the
> wall and continued to drink his essence.

The thing is, characters aren't cameras. They're experiencing this action, not watching it happen. And their experience flavors the action with meaning. So here's this action from Morticia's point of view.

> Morticia leaned forward. Her nostrils flared with the scent of Frank's blood, pulsing just below the skin of his neck. Her fangs lengthened and she sank them into a vein. The sweetness of blood washed over her tongue and poured down her throat. His moan aroused her further, and when he writhed within her grip, power rushed through her and she pinned him to the wall, drinking in the smell of his fear and relishing the rich taste of his essence.

Do you think Frank's experience of the very same action will feel the same as Morticia's? Hardly.

> Frank shrank back when Morticia leaned forward, panic pounding in his mind. She was . . . smelling him? Oh, God, she had fangs, and they grew as he watched. She struck and twin points of pain pierced his neck. Hot liquid trickled down— his blood? A moan crawked out of his throat and he writhed, pushing with all his strength to escape. As if he were a child, she jammed him against the wall with terrible power and sucked even more ferociously.

Now, I'm not claiming that the above examples are great writing—hey, I just pulled them out of the air. But I do think that the technique illustrated is valid—no, vital—to creating an experience for your reader. Describe, yes, but flavor the scene with how the character feels it, experiences it.

Even a color can have meaning. Which of these gives you experience versus information?

> Sheila's dress was blue.
> Sheila's dress was the same sleazy blue Steve's mother had worn whenever she went out to get drunk.

EXPERIENTIAL DESCRIPTION OF PEOPLE

The snapshot:

Tony enters the room and he smiles widely as he gazes at the two women there.

The scenario:

The two women are, respectively:

> Violet has just started dating Tony and has the hots for him.
> Virginia was Tony's last girlfriend who he ditched to go out with Violet.

Here's the description of Tony from **Violet's** POV:

> Tony strode into the room like the masterful man he was, his shoulders back, his chin up. Her pulse picked up speed when his oh-so-kissable lips smiled and she warmed, well, down there.

As for **Virginia:**

> Tony swaggered into the room like the conceited son of a bitch he was, swinging his padded

shoulders and looking down his nose. Her pulse pounded in her head when his shit-eating grin turned her face hot with a need to punch out his lights.

Here's an elegant use of this technique in *The Silver Swan,* by Benjamin Black. A woman watches a man who could simply be described as lean and lanky, but the author helps us perceive him through her eyes in a way that characterizes both of them.

What a lovely loose way he had of walking, leaning down a little way to one side and then the other at each long, loping stride he took, his shoulders dipping in rhythm with his steps and his head sliding backwards and forwards gently on its tall stalk of neck, like the head of some marvelous, exotic wading bird.

USE THE 5 SENSES EXPERIENTIALLY WHENEVER POSSIBLE

Flavor the perceptions a character gets from sight, hearing, smell, taste and touch with reactions and personality. To revisit a brief scene from the chapter on adverbs:

Jimmy crept across a room cluttered with shrunken heads. He was glad that the light of his candle was dim—all those tiny faces staring up at him were entirely too creepy. He set a foot down and winced at a crunch. He froze, listening for sounds of renewed pursuit. But only the scurrying of rats troubled the air, musty with the dust of the dead.

Rats?

Oh, fine.

Jimmy not only sees the skulls, he sees them as creepy, which is why he's glad the light is dim. A crunch causes a wince. The scurrying of rats he hears is troubling.

ON THE OTHER HAND

There are no rules. I feel obliged to point out that, while I think fiction that utilizes experiential description in key passages is stronger and more engaging, it isn't the only way to deliver a fascinating story.

The reason I feel obligated to point this out is that as I was working on this book, I picked up Stephen King's *The Eyes of the Dragon*. Published in 1988, it's King doing his thing with the classic fairy tale—the good prince and the bad prince, the evil magician, dragons . . .

And Stephen tells the tale from a surface third person point of view. His voice was the narrator's voice, never the character's, and once in a while he spoke directly to the reader. He didn't render the experience of the characters, and I was distant from the story, much more of an observer than a participant.

Because of King's voice and the fun of the tale, I had a great time. The distance from the story didn't matter, it was fun because I had a gifted storyteller's voice whispering in my ear.

Just sayin'.

However, that is not to say that the same story and the same characters couldn't have been more powerful illustrations of how to be a person if they had been written in a different way. That's the beauty of being a writer—you have an amazing amount of control over exactly what the reading experience will be: the reader's emotional involvement, her intellectual involvement, her takeaway.

It's your bus to drive, your road to take, just make the trip as much of an experience as you can.

Eliminate filters that distance a reader's experience

I HAVE ALWAYS HAD A PROBLEM with "he felt" and steered editing clients away from it, but hadn't realized that it was just one example of what are called "filters" until a reader on my blog pointed that out. She steered me to *Writing Fiction* by Jane Burroway. The book cites author/teacher John Gardner:

> "... the needless filtering of the image through some observing consciousness. The amateur writes: 'Turning, she noticed two snakes fighting in among the rocks.' Compare: 'She turned. In among the rocks, two snakes were fighting ...' Generally speaking—though no laws are absolute in fiction—vividness urges that almost every occurrence of phrases as 'she noticed' and 'she saw' be suppressed in favor of direct presentation of the thing seen."

Burroway points out that when you look *at* a character rather than *through* a character, you start to tell-not-show and rip us briefly out of the scene, out of the experience of the story.

Leslie Leigh, who writes the *Leslie's Writing Exercises* blog, put it well:

"Filters keep the reader from sinking comfortably into the fictional dream. One moment the reader is hunched over the POV character's shoulder, observing the world as if he is that character, seeing only what the character sees. But stumble across a 'filtered observation' and suddenly the reader finds himself looking at the character instead of with the character—watching the character as the character watches something else."

Actually, I think there are two kinds of filters:

1. **Action filters**—the kind Burroway talks about, placing a character's action between the detail you want to present and the reader.
2. **Body-part filters**—using a body part rather than the character to do the thing you want the reader-as-character to experience doing.

ACTION FILTERS

If the scene is clearly in the deep POV of a character, readers don't need to be told the character sees, hears, or smells something. When the "something" appears readers intuitively assume the POV character sees-hears-smells it.

Filters back the reader away from the character's experience by one step because the focus of the narrative becomes the character's action rather than the actual thing the character senses or does.

It turns out that action filters go beyond things seen—here's a narrative example:

Harvey heard the howl of a coyote. He went to the front door, opened it, and stuck his head out. He shivered when he felt the sting of the winter wind and ducked back inside. Then he noticed a second coyote's howl join the first. He decided to get the shotgun from above the fireplace mantle and scare them off.

Same scene without the filters:

A coyote howled outside. Harvey opened the front door and stuck his head out. He shivered when the winter wind stung his face and he ducked back inside. A second coyote's howl joined the first. He got the shotgun above the fireplace mantle to scare them off.

Here's a partial list of common verbs that can create distance between the reader and the story experience:

- he saw
- she heard
- he thought
- she touched
- he wondered
- she realized
- he watched
- he looked
- it seemed
- she felt or felt like
- he decided
- she noticed (a very common one)
- he noted
- it sounded or sounded like
- she was able to
- he managed
- she experienced

Body-part filters

A reader's mind reacts instantaneously to word stimuli—write "cat" and an image of a cat pops into the mind. Write "cat's paw" and an image of a cat's paw appears in a close-up. Therein lies the filter created by using body parts to do things in a story rather than using the character. As an action filter has a reader seeing the action, this kind of filter has the reader looking at a body part rather than being with the character in experiencing the story.

If you write "eyes," an image of eyes comes to mind: "His eyes searched wildly for a way out."

If you use a pronoun or a name, an image of the character comes to mind: "He searched wildly for a way out."

Literally, it's not his eyes that are doing the searching, it is the character. If what I write has you visualizing a pair of eyes moving jerkily from side to side, is that as true an image as getting you to visualize a man turning his head rapidly as he scans the area for an escape route?

Which serves the story better? Which delivers the character's experience? I think it's the image of the man. Consider these:

> Nervous about meeting Bob, Stephanie cupped her hand and her nose smelled her breath.

OR

> Nervous about meeting Bob, Stephanie cupped her hand and smelled her breath.

> Frightened by the kindergarten teacher, little Elsa shrank in her seat and her mouth sucked her thumb.

OR

> Frightened by the kindergarten teacher, little Elsa shrank in her seat and sucked her thumb.

His elbow smashed into the monster's face.

OR

He smashed his elbow into the monster's face.

His fingertips caressed her face.

OR

He caressed her face with his fingertips.

Examples from submissions to my blog:

> Keith stumbled. ~~His body~~ *He* pitched forward
> ~~Her body~~ *She* lurched forward and her hands flew up.
> ~~His arm~~ *He* recognized her touch.

Not all body parts in action are filters. It's perfectly okay to have a body part do something that is a part of what the character is experiencing. For example, is this right?

> Billy buckled his knees when Tom landed a punch on his jaw.

Nawww . . .

> Billy's knees buckled when Tom landed a punch on his jaw.

Avoid conclusion words

AUTHOR BARBARA D'AMATO FINDS consistent factors in the work of beginning writers that can stifle a promising narrative. One she talked about in a post for *The Outfit*, a multi-author blog by Chicago crime writers, struck me because it's something I'm constantly pointing out in my edits. I just didn't have this fine label for them that she used: "conclusion" words.

Barbara says she sees "too many 'conclusion' words: beautiful, arrogant, ugly, magnificent, ghastly, stately, scary, and so forth."

Here are a few more:

- handsome
- attractive
- momentous
- embarrassing
- fabulous
- powerful
- hilarious
- fascinating

When used as description, these conclusion words are *telling*, and they offer no real clue as to what the reader should be seeing. For example, what images come to mind when you read the following description?

Allyson was beautiful.

Any picture of Allyson has to be reader-generated and may have nothing to do with what the author intends. Beauty, being in the eye of the beholder, is subjective. You may think an anorexically thin Allyson to be beautiful while I think she should see a doctor. Steve may think that a woman with a good extra fifty pounds of love handles is beautiful while Roger thinks she should call Weight Watchers. And so on.

The difference between telling and showing usually boils down to the physical senses.

If the author wants us to think Allyson is beautiful, she needs to give us pictures that illustrate beauty, not labels.

Allyson moved with a ballerina's grace, and her slender figure made any clothing look good. Shoulder-length hair the color of dark chocolate framed a face that made Johnny think of a princess in a fairy tale, and he wanted to be the one to kiss lips that smiled and pouted and invited all at the same time.

That's not to say that you should avoid conclusion words. For example the word beautiful can be quite useful in characterizing. Here's a descriptive passage from my novel, *The Summer Boy*, in which two teenage boys are going to work on a ranch for the summer and go to a small log cabin that's to be their quarters.

Excitement grew in Jesse as they approached the cabin. A place all their own. No grown-ups.

Inside, they stood in a main room just big enough for a double bunk bed, a four-drawer dresser, two chairs beside a small table, and a little space left over to walk around. A battered old radio sat on the table, and an easy-going breeze wafted through the screened door and out the single side window.

A doorway into the bathroom revealed an old-fashioned tub with feet; a metal bar suspended from the ceiling encircled it with a shower curtain. Jesse stepped to the door and looked in. The toilet had a seat but no lid, the sink a medicine cabinet above it, but the mirror was cracked.

Beautiful.

So "conclusion" words can be useful when you use them to describe just that: a conclusion. Jesse concludes that the cabin is beautiful even though, to his mom, I'm certain it would be far from it. In this case, it helps to characterize Jesse.

In looking through submissions from writers for their use of "beautiful," I find examples that make Barbara's "conclusion" label clear.

It's a beautiful day, so we drive to Lyme Park.

Can't see the day, can you?

He gestures at a strikingly beautiful black woman sitting opposite him.

No picture there. Oh, we know the impact of the woman's appearance on our point-of-view character, but not what causes it. If we received a picture of the black woman, we'd learn what "beautiful" means to our POV character, and thus gain insight into his character. But in this case we learn nothing.

Here's an example where the conclusion word is at least followed by the description:

> They've got two little boys who are utterly beautiful—all huge blue eyes, blond hair and cheeky grins.

Here are especially common conclusion words:
- elegant
- shabby
- bizarre
- eerie
- weird (a common one)
- strange (another common one)
- eclectic
- large or small (also relative terms meaningless without a comparison)
- young or old (also relative terms meaningless without a comparison)

I suggest you do a search for the conclusion words from this section and any others you can think of and see if you've used them as description words—and then substitute the description.

Inhabit characters to imagine their experience

WHEN AN AUTHOR STORY-TELLS well, a reader comes to inhabit a character, seeing and feeling as the character does—identifying with him. This is a good thing because if a reader cares about what happens to a character, she is compelled to read more (as long as interesting things happen, of course).

I'm a "pantser"—a writer who creates by the seat of his pants with no outline, as opposed to "plotters" who plan ahead with an outline. I'm not one for creating character profiles that list everything from religion to shoe size. For me to generate a narrative that draws a reader into a character, I shoehorn myself into a character's head and play the scene from there to truly "see" actions and reactions that reflect the character's reality. Here's an example of how I applied this technique to introduce a new character and setting.

Going into the scene, all I knew was plot material: the character's name and his role as an antagonist. I knew that he was inside a vehicle in which he traveled and lived. I knew the outside of the vehicle was wooden, and that he was in a forest preserve outside of Chicago in wintertime. I didn't even know what kind of vehicle he was in or what he looked like. That was about it.

When I inserted myself into my character's head and looked around, the first thing I discovered was that the room he was in was paneled with oak, and that Oriental rugs covered the floor. Why? Because that's the way this character would want his living space—rich and opulent. As I looked more closely, I saw that the oak paneling bore carved scenes from the history of his people. And that led me to how to discover and describe the setting and character in ways that helped the reader feel something. The scene from *Hiding Magic*:

> Drago shivers, gathers *lledri,* and controls the flow of the life force to create a blanket of energy that hugs his skin and repels the cold. Warm light from kerosene lamps give the impression of comfort, but the cabin is unpleasantly chilly despite oaken wall panels and woolen Oriental rugs that insulate the hardwood floor. The pot-bellied woodstove in the corner tempts him, but a column of smoke can't be disguised, and the danger of discovery is too great so close to a *lessi* city acrawl with people like maggots in a carcass.
>
> He tests the chill of a wall panel with a fin-gertip and then traces the carving there, a scene of his ancestor Merlin deep in conversation with King Arthur. The artist portrayed Merlin as tall and lean, with a handsome beard that reaches his chest. Drago wishes he looked like the carv-ing instead of the balding, plump appearance he associates with a ruddy-cheeked butcher in a small-town grocery store. He suspects that the real Merlin looked much like he does, and the majesty portrayed on the panel is no more than a craftsman's imagination at work.
>
> Drago smiles at Merlin's reputation as a wizard, created by using *lledri* to do tricks that

looked like "magic" to medieval people. The *lessi* are so easily fooled.

He shakes his head at Merlin's brave but hopeless attempts to guide the *lessi* to a rational civilization. The wizard's blood runs true, though; Drago is close to creating his own remedy for a sick world. If he can just breach the last barrier, the *lessi's* constant attack on all he holds dear will vanish as if it had never been. Clan children will prosper, free of peril. The natural balance of the world will return, and the danger of global warming will vanish.

He strokes his moustache, the one thing he has in common with the carved image. Despite his centuries, his is still brown, as is what remains of his hair. If only he had found his *key* to rejuvenation before he reached his thirties and his scalp had become a bleak pink dome rising above a low hedge of hair. That he is stuck with his looks for the rest of his days is one of life's minor irritants.

None of this detail existed before I wrote the scene from within the character's head. This character became very human to me, with strong desires and a wistful wish that he still had his hair. (I hadn't really known that he was bald.) This is another example of experiential description that characterizes as well as depicts, and inhabiting a character is the key to writing experiential description.

Inhabit your characters so I can too.

With bright blue button eyes and a tuft of red hair, Baby Harry was adored from the second he arrived.

Use specifics to deliver what you intend

I ENJOYED IMMENSELY *The Modern Library Writer's Workshop* by Stephen Koch, a noted teacher and author. One of the reasons is that he talks about storytelling in ways that resonate with the way I approach it.

One point he made that sparked for me is that we (the authors) haven't actually told our stories until someone reads them. Koch writes:

> To be sure, the reader follows the writer's lead; but only the reader's imagination, collaborating with the writer's, can make anything happen on any page. It's the reader who visualizes the characters, the reader who feels and finds the forward movement of the story, the reader who catches and is caught in the swirls of suspense, rides the flow of meaning, and unfolds the whole kaleidoscope of perception.

Our readers can do that—must do that—to experience our stories. Or, rather, their version of our stories. Each reader will add shades to the meanings of words and expressions and actions. They'll never read the story we've imagined.

Still, we hope a reader will experience our stories the way we feel them, and we can get 'em close, damn close, close enough, with strong craft. One aspect of craft, in particular, is the tool we need: specific, concrete details and imagery.

It's what author and teacher Oakley Hall in *How Fiction Works* calls "specification," using concrete words and images rather than abstract words and generalizations. Here are wrong/right examples he gave.

> He was a big man with a beard.
> He filled the doorway, his beard glistening with curls.

> It was cold in the kitchen.
> She hunched her shoulders and rubbed her hands together against the chill in the kitchen.

> The crowd passed in the street.
> The street brimmed with the jostling of men in cloth caps and women in babushkas.

> It was raining.
> He drew his hand inside and licked rain-drops from his fingertips.

Specificity makes your visualizations vivid and alive by *showing* rather than *telling*. And specifics can help a reader "see" an image much closer to what you, the author, imagined.

Without specific, concrete images, your reader might imagine something you never intended and thus stray far from the story you wanted to tell. And it's important to make sure it's your story, not a walkabout made up of random associations to vague language.

Specificity has to do with writing for effect. Or maybe I should say writing to affect, to make sure the things that go on in your reader's mind are as close to your original thought as possible. Keep in mind the stimulus/response paradigm. What you put on the page—and only what you put on the page—kicks off neural responses in your reader that create what she thinks, imagines, understands, and feels.

But please don't overwrite—going on and on with details and including micro-specifics. Use only enough to keep the story moving ahead. When it comes to description, I'm with Stephen King, as expressed in his *On Writing*. To quote from his book,

> Look—here's a table covered with a red cloth. On it is a cage the size of a small fish aquarium. In the cage is a white rabbit with a pink nose and pink-rimmed eyes. In its front paws is a carrot upon which it is contentedly chewing. On its back, clearly marked in blue ink, is the numeral 8.

As King points out, the paragraph doesn't tell us what the cage is made of. Wire mesh? Steel rods? Glass? It doesn't tell us because it doesn't matter. Whatever the reader "sees" allows him to visualize the rabbit inside and the most important story part of the description, the number on its back.

Just as Koch did, King says that good description makes the reader a participant in the story. Exactly right. Crisp, tight description lets the reader fill in details, especially if they don't matter to the storyline.

Ways to describe a point-of-view character

ONE OF THE FIRST OPPORTUNITIES for a writer to break the spell he's weaving in the reader's mind is when the time comes to describe a character from within that character's point of view. You've seen the hackneyed "looks in a mirror" approach—although it works, it just isn't, well, good. But that's just one among many clumsy ways to add description. For example:

> She shook her long blond hair out of her eyes.

What's wrong with that? In my view, if you're deep in a character's point of view, experiencing the story as they do, you don't include things the character would not think or do in that situation—it's a break in point of view.

If your hair is in your eyes, the thought in your mind isn't to get your long blond hair out of your eyes, it's simply to get your hair out of your eyes. In this example, adding "long blond" is an authorial intrusion that distances the reader from the character.

MAYBE YOU DON'T EVEN NEED TO DESCRIBE A CHARACTER

Don't forget that you've got a reader out there, ready and eager to contribute to the vision. If you sketch in enough of a character's appearance for the reader to distinguish the character from others, the reader is perfectly capable of adding details to the picture in their mind. Being a participant in building the scene is part of the fun of reading.

When Elmore Leonard wrote in the *New York Times* about his ten rules of writing, he quoted a character from a John Steinbeck novel who says, "I don't like to have nobody tell me what the guy that's talking looks like. I want to figure out what he looks like from the way he talks."

Leonard goes on to say this:

> "In Ernest Hemingway's *Hills like White Elephants,* what do the 'American and the girl with him' look like?
>
> "'She had taken off her hat and put it on the table.'
>
> "That's the only reference to a physical description in the story, and yet we see the couple and know them by their tones of voice."

Readers will indeed fill in the picture without much help from you. While the author may know what a character looks like, maybe the reader doesn't need to quite so much.

If there's something remarkable about a character's appearance that affects the story, then there's a clear need to describe. A couple of examples that come to mind:

- A character is so beautiful that she or he draws a crowd wherever she or he goes.
- A man who is so ugly that he can't find work because people can't look at him.

But if you do need to describe a point-of-view character, there are several ways to do it.

The "character thinks about himself" approach:

In this example from *The Summer Boy*, we're in teenager Jesse's point of view. He's just remarked to his friend Dudley about a girl they've met who sparked a lot of interest in him.

> Dudley shrugged. "She was looking at you."
> Jesse could think of only one word for what she had seen—medium. Medium tall, medium brown hair, medium brown eyes, medium looks, medium build (if he could shed a couple pounds). Medium nobody.

Jesse's relatively low self-esteem gives the reader enough of a picture to go on. The passage then finds a way to give the reader Jesse's age within the context of describing the girl . . .

The "see a character through another's eyes" approach:

> Jesse had figured the rancher's daughter for sixteen when they met at the ranch house that morning, so he had a year on her. But she was already the kind of girl a boy undressed with his eyes.
> It wasn't her body that had started his mental peep show, although she was fun to look at. Lola was little, five feet tip to toe, if that. His gaze had roamed happily down and back up slender, tanned legs exposed by short shorts, but on top she was no Playmate of the Month.
> It was a boldness in her green eyes that promised the stuff of daydreams. And then her handshake had lingered, her fingertips trailing across his palm.

I feel that this technique is showing, via Jesse's feelings and reactions, rather than telling. The description of the girl characterizes both of them—it's much more than a simple snapshot, a list of features such as hair and eye color, height, weight, etc. Here's how Jesse's friend Dudley was described, using the "another's eyes" approach. Past history between the friends helps characterize and describe at the same time:

> Dudley moved in even slower motion. Big and powerful at six feet and on the fat side, every year the Wildcat football coach came after Dudley for the offensive line, and every year Dudley was too lazy for all that exercise. But his strength hadn't seemed to help today.

At this point in the narrative, the owner of the ranch the boys are working for arrives on the scene.

> Mister Braun fit Jesse's picture of a Texas rancher. Standing about eye to eye with Jesse, he was lean, his tan skin like a tight leather glove. The gray that peppered his black sideburns made him look old to Jesse, maybe as old as forty.
> The dust whitening his jeans looked like it belonged there, and the sweat darkening his shirt and straw cowboy hat looked like hard work. He wore heavy-duty high-top work shoes, not the boots Jesse had expected on a rancher.

You learn the boss's size—eye to eye with Jesse, who was "medium"—and have a picture of a middle-aged, lean man. But you also know something about his personality—he works hard enough to sweat a lot and doesn't mind getting dirty.

Descriptions can be lean (and I think should be, most of the time), but sometimes, if the character's appearance is a factor in the story because of how others react to her, I look for a way to build more of a picture. Here are two pieces from my novel, *Gundown (2015)*, that describe Jewel, a woman in her twenties.

THE "CHARACTER REACTS TO OTHERS" APPROACH:

Murphy's piggy eyes stumbled across Jewel when she closed on him. His gaze went for its usual tour of her body—yeah, she was wearing a scoop-neck top and a mini-skirt, but what the hell, couldn't a girl enjoy a spring day without some slob feeling her up with his eyeballs?

Okay, now we know how she's dressed, and our imaginations fill in a woman shapely enough to provoke such attention. The action continues with. . .

THE "CHARACTER REACTS TO EVENTS" APPROACH:

A breeze reeking of car exhaust swirled between the skyscrapers, but she liked its touch. She turned her face to the spring sun and imagined she could feel it adding new cocoa dots to the spray of freckles on her brown skin.

Now we know, sort of, the color of her skin. And something about her personality, a certain sensuality. But wait, there's more . . .

THE "LOOKS AT A REFLECTION" APPROACH:

A character looking into a mirror is a hoary and clichéd

approach to showing what a character looks like, but I think you can do this as long as it reflects a true point-of-view response (and, if possible, avoids the use of a mirror).

> She stopped at a restaurant window to eye a cupcake display. In her reflection, her ice-blue eyes—donated by some honky ancestor—jumped out at her. So did her scar, a three-inch trail curving down from high on her cheekbone.
>
> She gave her body the once-over like Murphy had. Still lookin' good . . . Wait a minute, was that a little bit of extra tummy? She turned sideways. Damn, gettin' poochy. Should she diet? Exercise? Both? She sucked her gut in and walked on.

This last descriptive part combines the "reflection" approach with the "thinks about self" technique in a believable and natural way. Her reflection is used to provoke thoughts that characterize (i.e. her concern about her figure) without the author telling the reader details about her figure. The description of her scar is necessary to motivate character reactions to her that come along later.

Color narrative to characterize

WHAT A CHARACTER SAYS, thinks, and does is guided by personality, needs, perceptions, abilities and limitations. Of course. But I believe a writer should take that principle a level deeper: in deep third person point of view, even expository narration should reflect the character's personality, should be colored by the character's persona in a way that creates a distinct voice in your reader's ear.

That portion of the story should read as if the character has composed the narrative, not the author. Done well, once a reader is introduced to a character she will recognize a character's narrative even if the character is not named. Each character is a different color on your narrative pallet.

The key to doing this was brought home to me when a critique partner said about a novel in progress that she was helping with, "I love the change of vocabulary accompanying the change in POV." She referred to the word choices in the exposition part of the narrative, not the dialogue, and had put her finger on the root technique for flavoring in a way that I hadn't thought of.

It's the words, stupid.

How many popular novels fail to do this? I see them; don't you? While dialogue may differ (often not by much), exposition is flat and non-differentiated. But it could be different. I say it should be.

Here's an example of coloring a narrative from a mystery novel that takes place in the old West. When it shifts from one point of view to another, so does the voice of the narrative.

> Wood thunked on wood and Zach whirled, his finger tightening against the trigger. In the doorway to the spare room stood a boy of about ten. A boy propped on a crutch, his left leg hanging limp. A boy with Tom's long, serious face, his sandy hair, and his hazel eyes, eyes that fastened on Zach's. They widened. "Father?"
>
> Zach turned to the woman. "Where's Tom Duval?"
>
> She swayed and braced herself with a hand on the window sill. She stared at him.
>
> He had to have an answer. "Who are you?"
>
> She lifted her chin and leveled golden eyes at him.
>
> "His widow."
>
> * * *
>
> Amber felt him lookin' at her. Like all men did.
>
> Except for the fancy city suit, he was the spittin' image of Tom. Same stocky body, strong-looking, the hazel eyes with arching brows that made his gaze seem like it was coming after her.
>
> Why in hell did he have to show up? A few more days and she'd have been out of this inferno.

Here are two characters in my speculative thriller, *Gundown*.

A tiresome clump of a half-dozen gang jerks swaggered toward Jake with cocky menace, semi-automatic pistols visible. The gangbangers blocked most of the sidewalk, forcing people to step off the curb or sidle along a building front. Jake locked his gaze onto the eyes of the guy in the center and walked straight at him.

The kid kept his cool as they came together, but one stride from colliding he dropped his gaze and sidestepped. Never slowing, Jake cut through.

He focused on what he knew of the attorney general. He'd heard from his old contacts in Justice that Marion Smith-Taylor was honest and devoted to the law, and that she hated the under-the-table deal-making of politics. He had, too . . . once upon a time.

* * *

Two white dudes slouched against a gun store smacked kisses at her. A green stripe ran down the center of the blond's buzz-cut hair, and a red do-rag decorated the smaller guy's shaved head—he cupped his balls and licked his lips. Ugh. Jewel lengthened her stride, her mini-skirt riding high.

They pushed off from the store and swung into step on each side of her. Green-Stripe crowded against her. His sour stink assaulted her, and the skin on her arms goose-bumped. He said, "Hey, Brown Sugar."

She wanted to say "I'm not your sugar," but no, just keep going. Staring straight ahead, she said, "There's a cop back there."

He laughed. "Yeah. Murphy."

Wishing she wasn't wearing heels, she broke into a run and darted between a couple holding hands.

Color narrative with the same vocabulary and style as a character's dialogue and you'll increase your odds of delivering the character's experience directly to your reader. Each character's turn on the stage will resonate as a person, not just a puppet you've trotted out to roll the plot wheel.

Stagecraft: don't trip over your imaginings

STAGING IS HOW ACTION unfolds or how a character interacts with the setting. It's a necessary part of description, and one in which writers are particularly prone to lapses. Because they see the action so clearly in their minds, it's easy to leave out vital clues that the reader needs. Or sometimes it's the opposite—a character is racing through a high-action scene and the writer fails to see the action clearly. A writer can be so focused on the outcome she wants that she unwittingly bends possibility until it breaks.

The logic problems that bad staging creates raise two issues that become especially damning if the reader is an agent or acquisitions editor:

- You lose credibility with the reader.
- You confuse the reader, which can mean that she has to break out of the story to figure out what's going on, or might just stop reading altogether.

But there's a way to get your staging right. Slip into a character's skin, look around, and go through his motions. If you act out the action in your mind (much different than simply writing a description of it), you can keep it real. And sometimes it's a good idea to get off your chair and physically go through the actions you're describing.

Following are examples adapted from edits I've done. First I'll give you the excerpt, and then the comment I gave in the edit.

> An elderly man shuffled toward them. He wore a
> hospital johnnie that dangled open in the back.

Comment: If he's coming toward the point-of-view character, the POV guy can't see that it dangles open in the back—you need to either cut this or fix the staging so that it can be seen. See if you find this one confusing.

> Looking over at him, she could not remember
> if she had ever made love in the afternoon, in
> a room with the shades up. A time when it did
> not matter if the sun had set, or the blinds were
> drawn, or the door locked to ward off children.
> But now, watching the leaves come down, she
> could not remember such a time.

Comment: At this moment you have her looking over at him as he sleeps, not watching the leaves and then suddenly she's watching leaves. Suggest you have her turn her gaze back to the leaves before her concluding thought.

Next, the character is blindfolded in a place she has never been.

> As the man who had been holding her walked
> away, she could hear his feet echoing down the hall.

Comment: You had written this as if she could know he went down a hall, but it has to be a question because she can't see. Thought-starter: When the man who had been holding her walked away, she could hear his footsteps echo—down a hall?

In the following example, the character has picked up a basket on his front porch that contains a baby and taken it inside. Then this happens . . .

> Holding the basket in my lap, I pulled the blanket aside.

Comment: Is he sitting somewhere? The living room? Kitchen? You need to set the scene a little so the reader can picture the character in action. Another thought: a basket large enough to hold a baby would be pretty big to put in your lap. Suggest he either set it on the floor or on the kitchen table.

Next, brevity creates confusion.

> The Chevy glided over the bumps in the rutted road. Darkness had fallen as he slowed on the unfamiliar road looking for her house.

Comment: There's something wacky about the sense of this staging of darkness coming and the slowing of the car. It means that darkness came in/during the time it took him to slow down. Either darkness falls far more quickly where he lives than it does on my part of the planet, or he took an awfully long time to slow down. You need to adjust the "reality" of this darkening.

> Once safely inside her flat on the fourth floor, she went to open her bedroom window. She recoiled behind the curtain when she saw a long shadow on the pavement below recede into darkness. She recognized him.

Comment: She saw only a shadow and yet she recognized him? Doesn't seem possible, especially if she is four stories up and it is dark outside. Need to rethink what the staging is here if you want her to see the guy well enough to recognize.

Moral: inhabit characters so you don't trip over the scenery. Act out the action in your mind to reveal gaps and impossibilities.

Second moral: find sharp "other eyes" to help spot goofs you can't see.

Watch out for the incredibles

THE "INCREDIBLES" APPEAR when you have a character do something either improbable or impossible. I see manuscripts peppered with little impossibilities and improbabilities, although I suspect that many readers would never notice them. At least consciously. Even if not noticed, they can work to take a reader out of your story and damage its credibility. The suspension of disbelief may be destroyed. Here are some from work I've edited:

> He clenched his teeth and said, "I could kill you."

> "You always wanted to fly, Erin," he said through gritted teeth.

Okay, now you try clenching or gritting your teeth and saying anything intelligible. Don't fudge, keep your teeth clamped together. You'll note that not only can you not talk very well, but a character would look darned silly doing it. I find it unrealistic to portray a character talking like this.

Writers have argued with me that it's possible, and yes, it is. Sort of like what a ventriloquist does. But have you ever, really, said something through tightly clenched teeth? I haven't, and I don't think a character would. If you want clenched or gritted teeth, separate them from the dialogue.

> He clenched his teeth and then said, "I could kill you."

Here's a subtle impossibility.

> I bent down, gingerly touching the small gray bone.

The sense of the sentence is that he touched the bone as he bent down, but that's not right because the bone is on the ground and he can't touch it until after he bends down. More accurately:

> I bent down and gingerly touched the small gray bone.

Here's a tidy impossibility:

> He snarled silently.

A snarl is a sound, so you can't snarl silently. Your mouth can curl as if snarling, though.

A perennial favorite is using "eyes" in a silly way.

> We stood for a long moment, our eyes locked.

So these people put their faces so impossibly close together that their eyes locked together? The writer means "gazes."

> Arlene shifted her eyes to the piles of vegetables.

Really, eyes are much more functional when they stay in your head, don't you think? Another time when "gaze" was called for.

Here's a different "eye" thing:

> She wiggled to a sitting position, her eyes sleepy but bright, tugging at the neck of her footy-pajamas.

This sentence has this person's eyes tugging at the neck of her jammys. Weird.

How people use their bodies often suffers from a case of the impossibles. In the following example, the writer could clearly see the action in her mind, she just failed to get it on paper phrased in a clear way.

> I wrapped myself around him and we dropped to our knees.

This leads me to picture someone wrapping their arms and legs around someone else, right? And then they both drop to their knees? Naw.

> I watched Ellen and her friend drive back to Studio City in their BMW as I waited for someone to answer my call.

Unless this character is in a helicopter or hot air balloon, he/she can't watch someone drive to another city. The writer really meant "depart for" Studio City.

> The voices began, too low to be heard.

If the character knows the voices begin, then he hears them.

The writer meant that the words couldn't be understood because the voices were so low.

> (a man looks at a diapered baby) I saw instantly
> that the baby was wet.

Nope. You can feel whether or not a diaper is wet, but you can't really see it, especially nowadays with disposable diapers. These illustrate the need for fresh eyes. Sharp, picky eyes. Eyes that do not leave heads but instead stay put and search for the incredibles.

Overwriting: the attack of killer verbiage

SOME WRITERS NEW TO THE TASK of writing a novel or memoir
put in every possible nuance and detail of a scene or action—and
drown their pace and tension in a sludge of words. Invisible and
deadly, overwriting can suffocate a narrative.

Overwriting is insidious, and can grow just a word or two at
a time. Here are two examples from a client's work:

> He tasted her in his mouth. *(Where else
> would he taste her?)*

> Her heart clenched in her chest. *(Better there
> than in her purse, I guess.)*

What pains me are far worse examples in published novels.
Take the following trudge from *The Experiment* by John Darnton.

The scene: a woman enters a darkened bedroom. In the bed
sleeps a man who she assumes is her love interest. Spreading
minutiae like a blanket of kudzu, Darnton writes . . . and writes
. . . and writes . . .

> She thought that perhaps she should try to
> take a nap, too; the trip home had exhausted her.

> She walked around the bed, sat in a chair and unstrapped her shoes and took them off, placing them to one side. She stood up and unzipped her dress, letting it fall to the floor in a heap and bent down to pick it up and drape it over the back of the chair. She slipped her thumbs into the waist of her panties and slid them down her legs, placing them over the dress. Then she unfastened her bra and placed it on top. From the bed, she heard his breathing shift as he moved to a different level of sleep.
>
> She walked to the right side of the bed, lifted the sheet and slipped underneath, pulling it up to her chin. The cotton felt cool to her skin.

Does the word "turgid" come to mind? If not, see a therapist immediately. Trust me on this: the entire purpose of this passage was to get the woman into the bed. Her method of disrobing had absolutely no bearing on anything that had gone before or anything that happened afterward. Nothing. Nada. Zilch.

It didn't matter that she walked around the bed. Or sat in a chair. Or where she placed her discarded shoes. Or what she did with her dress or bra. Nor did her panty-removal process have any bearing—the person in the bed was asleep, and there was no sexual intent to the scene. And it didn't matter which side of the bed she got into, either. Don't get me started on other deficiencies in this dawdle. In the example above, all that verbiage boils down to this:

> Exhausted by the trip home, she thought she should try a nap. She undressed, slipped underneath the sheet and pulled it up to her chin, the cotton cool on her skin.

Here's a technique that might have helped Mr. Darnton avoid his logorrhea—read your narrative aloud. If, at some point, you detach and drift, your voice a drone in the background while your mind searches for something interesting to think about, your narrative has been binge expositing, and you need to apply the cure—vigorous exercise of the delete key.

But overwriting slips in with shorter verbiage, too. Some examples from submissions to my blog—the italics are what I added after making the deletion:

> "Seriously? I thought you had something to tell me." I said ~~leaning against the banister~~. *Where he leaned had nothing to do with what's happening.*

> Feeling a touch on his sleeve, he turned and his smile disappeared. ~~Looking first left then right, he~~ **He** ~~angrily~~ spat, "I told you to leave me alone!" *How he looks around matters not, just his anger does.*

> "This is Matt Lanier. ~~I'm returning the call I received earlier this evening.~~ My father, Ray Lanier is there." Matt ~~turned and~~ looked out his living room window, bracing for ~~the psychological impact of~~ what he was about to hear. *Clutter.*

> Ramon stood under the awning and watched the gringo breathe. ~~He could just see the man's chest rise and fall amid the spattering raindrops. A cigarette hung limp from his mouth, its tip adding a wisp of smoke to the moist air.~~ *Atmospheric, but totally not needed.*

~~Leaning against the front of the desk to her right he~~ **He** pointed to the last entry. "This is what the duke was here for." *Again, where he leaned has no effect on the story.*

Alex ~~removed the cap from the bottle, and~~ poured the little white pills into her hand, . She ~~closed her fist tightly, and~~ stared past the waiting glass of water at the intricate lace pattern of the tablecloth. *Excess detail slows the narrative.*

Fidel scowled ~~at the interruption~~, but then shook off his annoyance as he conceded ~~to himself~~ that he had been delaying. He owed them a decision. "We go," he said ~~without turning away from the window.~~ *Words that are just not needed.*

Bracing herself, Mara ~~crossed the short distance to the door and~~ pulled **the door** ~~it~~ open. *The distance to the door didn't matter in the story.*

I suspect some of these might have been spotted if the writer had tried reading the narrative aloud. I've learned that I need to do it for my own work despite all the editing I do for others.

Dialogue techniques

JUST AS A NOVEL WITHOUT description would be a radio script, a novel without dialogue would be a word-picture book. To state the obvious, dialogue characterizes, illustrates, and moves action. So we needn't get into that.

But many writers find it difficult to craft smooth, credible, crisp dialogue. Some of the hazards are:

- Dialogue tags gone wrong
- Naked dialogue
- Over-use of "with"
- Bassackwards delivery of the sound of a speech

Well, this section can help.

Tags: a game writers shouldn't play

BECAUSE EACH OF US HAS a lifetime of experience with talking, writing dialogue in a novel seems like it should be easy, and maybe it is for some writers. But for others it's the weakest part of their narrative. Three common flaws I see in beginning work are:

- Botched use of dialogue tags
- Lack of effective action beats
- Explaining the dialogue instead of showing it happening

Here's a snippet of dialogue guaranteed to make you cringe:

"Please don't do that," he articulated.
"What?" she interrogated.

Okay, perhaps that's a touch over the top. But how many times have you seen dialogue tags like the following?

Melissa turned to Irving. "Why don't you zip up your pants?" she asked.
He shrugged. "Air conditioning," he replied.

What's with "she asked" and "he replied"? The question mark clearly tells the reader that a question was asked, and the response is clearly a reply, and the reader damn well knows what they were. Yet "she asked" and the ever-popular "he replied" clog thousands of pages like verbal cholesterol.

When it comes to dialogue tags, a couple of clichés should be applied:

1. Less is more.

2. KISS—Keep It Simple, Stupid

Tags can tangle dialogue and slow pace; their absence can smooth and accelerate. Over-explanatory tags (he huffed, she whimpered) create lazy writing; replacing them with action or description gives the words meaning and tone that involves the reader, creates pictures, and enhances emotional effect.

Here are just a few of the words often used as dialogue tags that shouldn't be:

> hissed, laughed, nodded, belched, surmised, growled, snorted, snarled, wept, exclaimed, begged, implored, suggested, noted

If you try saying a line of dialogue with "sound" tags such as "hissed" and "snarled" you'll soon see why they don't work—you can't say anything intelligible when hissing, snarling, etc.

Rarely is there a need for a dialogue tag other than "said," even with a question. A *Writer's Digest* article pointed out that "said is a word that is noted but not noticed." For example, there's no need to use "asked" or "interrogated" or "queried" if you write:

> Farnsworth said, "Where do you think the monster is hiding?"

The reader understands that Farnsworth has asked a question—that's what question marks are for. To add tonality, use description and action, and remove the "said." For example:

Farnsworth's voice came from under the couch in a whisper that ended with a sob. "Where do you think the monster is hiding?"

To illustrate minimizing dialogue tags in a scene, here's an excerpt from *Gundown*. In the scene, Marion Smith-Taylor, the U.S. Attorney General, is calling her office from out of town. See what you think, tag-wise.

Time enough for one last Hail Mary—she took out her cell phone and auto-dialed her office.

Suzanne Fisher answered. "Ms. Smith-Taylor's office, how may I help you?"

Marion pictured Suzanne, not in an office outfit but bundled up in her pale blue terry-cloth robe, blond hair tousled, fair cheeks flushed. If Marion had her druthers, Suzanne would be helping her to a tumbler of Scotch—but that would have to wait until she was home. "Hi, Suze, it's me."

"I was just thinking about you."

That was one of the things Marion loved about Suzanne—no games, she just said how she felt. "Me, too. Listen, they're about to get here. Anything on the Alliance from Joe Donovan or Sally Arnold?"

"No word."

"Damn." She'd been praying for better information on the Oregon situation before the meeting. But she wasn't surprised; Joe and Sally had been less than helpful for months. Something had changed with them. "If you hear from them in the next hour, call."

"I will."

Damn. Damn-damn-damn.

Seven speeches from two characters and not a single dialogue tag. And I'll bet you didn't get lost.

Enough articulated?

WHAT ABOUT "HE THOUGHT?"

A common way of indicating the thoughts of a character is to signal with "he thought" and then include the thought in italics or use quotes.

But italics can be hard to read, quotes can lead to confusing thoughts with dialogue, and writing "he thought" isn't really necessary.

When you're using a deep third person point of view, you can include a character's thoughts as a part of the narrative via internal monologue. Very simply, it's the thought expressed in the same person and tense as the rest of the narrative. The reader will understand that it is a thought of the character. For example, in this scene from *Gundown* the protagonist, Jake, sees a woman being assaulted in an alley:

Jake looked north toward his waiting appointment.

Back into the alley.

The woman staggered her attacker with a kick to his leg. He slapped her, and then had to dodge a knee aimed at his crotch. Girl had guts.

"Girl had guts" is a snippet of internal monologue showing Jake's thought. It's a lot quicker and cleaner than this:

Jake thought, *The girl has guts.*

Here's a passage from *Gundown* with a couple of instances of internal monologue from the woman who was being attacked. This happens after Jake intervenes and stops the attack. We're now in her point of view.

> Jewel settled herself down. Her mama had always said, "In this world, you got to be hard. Ain't nobody there for you but you." Hallelujah, Mama.
> She'd been lucky today. She felt compelled to thank the guy, even if he was white—Mama'd taught her manners, too. Jewel hurried after him, trying to arrange her torn top into decent coverage, but one tit or the other kept falling out. Great, now she had to walk down Michigan Avenue with her boobs hanging out. And wouldn't they love it back at the office.

Here, "Hallelujah, Mama" is internal monologue. And so is

> Great, now she had to walk down Michigan Avenue with her boobs hanging out. And wouldn't they love it back at the office.

In *Self-editing for Fiction Writers*, authors Renni Browne and Dave King give a good example of this technique, which they call "interior monologue."

> Big Jim Billups fondled the .38 in his pocket, waddled over to the back of his truck, and spat. Could've stopped the whole damn thing last night—they don't carry no guns. What was the use of doing a job if you didn't do a good one?

He rocked, shifting his weight from one leg to another and spat again. The sound of the marchers was closer now. Soon it would be time.

As Browne and King point out, readers move easily from Big Jim's actions to his thoughts and back again without being aware of what they're doing. Renni and Dave's chapter on interior monologue gives excellent guidelines on the artful use of the technique.

Cook up some tasty beats

Naked dialogue, just speeches all by themselves, does only part of the job of delivering the experience of a scene. In life and in books dialogue doesn't happen in a vacuum—it happens in the midst of movement, body language, pauses for thought, and more. To bring dialogue to life, create "beats"—action, description, or thoughts interwoven with dialogue—to invisibly accomplish a number of vital storytelling tasks, including:

- Advancing the story
- Increasing tension
- Illuminating character
- Identifying speakers without having to use dialogue tags
- Adding meaning to speeches that wouldn't otherwise be there
- Breaking up long strings of quotations to avoid a staccato effect and to create a pleasing rhythm
- Creating pictures in the reader's mind of what's going on (Construe "picture" to include time [pace], scents, sensations, and sounds as well as action and physical description.)

Here's an example of a beat that does one of those things and yet is a waste of words. The scene is from a published novelist's first draft of a new story: a man and a woman sit at a table in a café, talking about a woman (his wife/her friend) who has been missing for over a week. In the course of the conversation in the woman's point of view, this happens:

> A man from the next table asked to borrow the extra chair to my right. As I nodded, Robert said, "I have not told you everything."
> "What?"
> "Her car was found abandoned in Stewart State Park."
> "Oh my God! When? How long after . . ."

The solo beat at the beginning did inject action into the scene . . . but it had nothing to do with story—it was "activity," not storytelling action. It didn't bear on the subject of the conversation, nor the people talking. It had no impact on the scene. An absolute waste of words.

The dialogue that follows it suffers due to a lack of beats. How about a little body language when Robert confesses he hasn't told his listener everything? Or a reaction when the narrator learns fraught information?

> Robert shifted his gaze away from me. "I have not told you everything."
> How like the man to withhold information.
> "What?"
> "Her car was found abandoned in Stewart State Park."
> "Oh my God!" Fear for my missing friend jolted through me. "When? How long after . . ."

Here's what each of those beats accomplished:
- The first told you who was speaking and

it also gave characterization and nuance to his speech.
- The second is internal monologue that adds characterization for both people.
- The last one injects emotion, information, and more characterization.

Let's beat up some more dialogue. Here's part of a scene from *Hiding Magic* stripped naked, all of the beats removed. In this scene, KB, a law enforcement officer, reports to her superior, and she expects him to praise her for what she'd done the day before.

Captain Berman's door is open, as usual. His white-haired head is bent over a stack of paperwork, as usual. Adrenaline pumps her up, and she taps on the doorframe and goes in. The office is too warm, as usual; the radiator must be cranked all the way open.

"Take a seat, Lieutenant. So, you think you found a subject of interest."

"Yessir!"

"Did you see it with the thermal imaging device?"

"I did, sir."

"Did you record it?"

"Ah, no, sir."

"I see. You say it changed appearance on three occasions?"

"From a youngish woman to an older woman, then to a hick, then to a girl. Yessir."

"Did any of your team see these apparitions?"

"Schultz saw it come in. Martinez saw it on the stairs, and Bailey saw it come out."

"After receiving your email, I asked your team for their input. Schultz didn't see a face."

"No, ah, he didn't get a good look. But he saw the glow in the camera."

"I see. No one else saw the older woman?"

"Not before she, uh, changed into a farmer."

You learn things, but there's no tension, no depth, you can't see a damn thing, and there's no rhythm—it's like a radio machine-gunning words at you. The full narrative follows—note that there's not a single use of a dialogue tag.

Captain Berman's door is open, as usual. His white-haired head is bent over a stack of paperwork, as usual. Adrenaline pumps her up, and she taps on the doorframe and goes in. The office is too warm, as usual; the radiator must be cranked all the way open.

He looks up and nods. No smile. "Take a seat, Lieutenant."

The old fart is old-fashioned and formal, so maybe he's not gonna come right out with her attaboy. Sitting, she tells herself to be patient, something that never comes easy.

He signs a piece of paper, places it in an out box, leans back, laces his fingers over his belly, and gazes at her. "So, you think you found a subject of interest."

She smiles. "Yessir!"

"Did you see it with the thermal imaging device?"

Inside, she smirks at his fussy way of talking. "I did, sir."

"Did you record it?"

Oh, shit. She'd been too excited. "Ah, no, sir."

"I see." He leans forward and studies a print-out of her email. "You say it changed appearance on three occasions?"

"From a youngish woman to an older woman, then to a hick, then to a girl. Yessir."

"Did any of your team see these apparitions?"

Can't the old idiot read? "Schultz saw it come in. Martinez saw it on the stairs, and Bailey saw it come out."

"After receiving your email, I asked your team for their input." He picks up a printout. "Schultz didn't see a face."

"No, ah, he didn't get a good look." Why does she feel like she's on trial? "But he saw the glow in the camera."

"I see." He reads more. "No one else saw the older woman?"

"Not before she, uh, changed into a farmer."

The beats give pace to the conversation and much, much more. Through the beats you experienced:

- His chilly greeting when she expects warmth, and then his dawdling even though she is anxious (finishing with papers, leaning back, lacing his fingers)
- Her smugness (the old fart was old-fashioned)
- Her eagerness (she smiled)
- Her low opinion of him (smirked at his fussy way of speaking to her)
- Her realization of a mistake she's made (too excited to record the suspect)
- His calm, steady approach (studied a printout)

- More of her disrespect (couldn't the old idiot read?)
- His steady pursuit (he picked up a printout and read it)
- Her increasing anxiety (was she on trial here?)

You get a sense of escalating tension in KB. The scene continues to build from here and ends with her feeling defeated, angry, and near tears when she'd begun the scene expecting praise. And it is the beats that take you there.

Not every line in dialogue gets a beat—that'll wear a reader out. Every beat is tied to characterization and/or giving a picture of what is going on. The beats utilize physical action and internal monologue (Couldn't the old idiot read?) to add depth and context to the spoken words.

The beats help pace the exchange, creating pauses (signed a piece of paper, placed it in an out box, leaned back, laced fingers, etc.) and emphasis (reading from something, etc.). Although there are no dialogue tags, you always know who's speaking and how they deliver their speeches.

The other cool thing about using beats is that it avoids the third most common dialogue flaw, explaining the dialogue with "with."

Don't say it with "with"

I HAVE A PET PEEVE when it comes to a certain kind of description in dialogue. It's this type of statement:

> He gazed at the painting. "Marvelous," he said
> with satisfaction.

My feeling is that the "he said with" construction signals lazy, ineffective dialogue. I went to *Self-Editing for Fiction Writers* to see what Renni Browne and Dave King have to say about it. While they didn't focus on the use of "with" in this way, it does fall within a craft no-no: explaining dialogue. Their position: don't do it.

Mine, too.

For one thing, it's telling, not showing. The example above is just that—telling the reader what the character's emotion is, not showing the emotion.

Saying it with "with" is lazy writing because good dialogue shouldn't have to be explained. Both the words and the action surrounding it should show emotion and nuance.

What if the example above went something like the following instead:

He gazed at the painting and then smiled. "Marvelous."

Written that way, I think the reader understands an even more complex array of emotion—pleasure, admiration, satisfaction—without using an iota of telling.

Following are examples of "withage" from samples sent to me and from client manuscripts:

"Dialogue," she said with a huge grin.

Clumsy. You say things with your mouth, for one thing.

Instead:

A grin stretched across her face. "Dialogue."

Note that you don't need a "she said" when you use an action beat in this way.

"Dialogue," he said with such hope in his voice.

Nope. What does "hope" in a voice sound like? I can't imagine it. Show me his emotion with behavior. What about this one?

"Dialogue," she said with a grin that couldn't help but make you smile back.

This is still "said with" and a complicated explanation of dialogue. What if it went this way?

She said, "Dialogue," and then flashed a grin that couldn't help but make you smile back.

There's more than a "said with" troubling the following narrative, including eyes that "dart" around.

> "Dialogue," he said with his eyes darting around looking for hidden spies in the bushes.

Instead, how about:

> His gaze darted over the bushes as he looked for hidden spies. "Dialogue."

The following example tries to show me an attitude rather than tell me about it, but it's still driving in reverse.

> "Dialogue," Farnsworth said with the assurance of a bridge player laying down the ace of trump.

Isn't his attitude clearer if you simply turn it around?

> With the assurance of a bridge player laying down the ace of trump, Farnsworth said, "Dialogue."

Come to think of it, "assurance" is still telling, isn't it? Wouldn't the reader get it if the narrative said this?

> Like a bridge player laying down the ace of trump, Farnsworth said, "Dialogue."

Another aspect of "said with" is that it suggests that characters do things that are not really possible.

> "Dialogue," he said with a shrug of his shoulders.

Unless you're using sign language, the only part of your body that actually says things is your mouth. When characters say things with a shrug or a scowl or a look, it bothers me.

By the way, the example also exhibits over-writing: the phrase "of his shoulders" is not needed. People don't shrug with any other part of their anatomy, and it suffices to say:

He shrugged. "Dialogue."

Note that a nine-word bit of narrative dropped to just three words and became more effective.

There's another problem with "said with"—the *way* the dialogue is said *follows* the speech. It's backward. Here come more real-life examples of using "said with." There's extra space between each example for you to write in how you would show the emotions instead of telling about them with "with."

It'll mean more if you actually do the rewriting.

"Dialogue," Steve said with contempt.

"Dialogue," I said with a bit of irritation in my voice.

"Dialogue," Ralph said with disgust.

"Dialogue," he said with obvious pride.

"Dialogue," Peggy said with a little belligerence.

"Dialogue," she said with delight.

"Dialogue," he said with a dull incurious inflection.

"Dialogue," he said with pretended anger.

"Dialogue," he said with seriousness befitting the formality.

Then there are the ones that try to blend action with speaking in ways that don't really work.

"Dialogue," she said with a giggle.

Not really. People giggle when they giggle and speak when they speak, but not at the same time. Instead, separate the action for a clearer picture and crisper dialogue.

She giggled. "Dialogue."

More examples from real manuscripts—in each case, think about how much more effective the dialogue portion would be if the action that characterizes it came first, and write your solution below it.

"Dialogue," Andrea said with her face screwed up.

"Dialogue," Byron said with a sideways look at me.

"Dialogue," she said with a wicked grin.

"Dialogue," she said with a worried look.

"Dialogue," she said with an admiring look.

"Dialogue," he said with just the hint of a smile.

"Dialogue," Susan said with a sigh.

"Dialogue," Pete said with a chuckle in his voice.

"Dialogue," she said with a frown.

"Dialogue," he said with a fixed stare.

So, I say with determination, your dialogue will be far more effective if you show emotion rather than explain it and place your illustrations before the dialogue so that the reader can apply the flavoring at the right time.

My advice? Search for "said with" and "asked with" and see if you can't do a better job of showing rather than telling.

Deliver the sound of dialogue

WHAT'S WEAK ABOUT this bit of narrative?

> "Hellooooo." The voice sounded ancient, an old
> lady maybe.

Description of the sound and character of a speech after it
has happened is a subset of explaining dialogue. It may not be
as obvious in a narrative, but I feel that it takes a step back from
writing for effect, away from creating the experience of the action
and dialogue in the reader's mind.

Maybe it's just me, but I feel that if you want a reader to
experience how a character sounds or says a line, the clue has
to come before the speech. When the description of the delivery
comes after the fact, it's merely information. To have the experience, the reader would have to backtrack and re-imagine the
speech, and no one does that—we're all moving forward to what
happens next. In our example, you get closer to the experience
if it's written this way:

> The woman's voice sounded ancient, maybe an
> old lady. "Hellooooo."

There's still a bit of telling to think about with this example (taken from a real manuscript): what does "sounded ancient" really mean? As a reader, you have to interpret that, don't you? You have to call up what an "old" voice might sound like, and then fill in the blanks. And you probably did that just fine. But what if the writer had described the sound of the voice instead?

> The woman's voice rasped and quivered, maybe an old lady. "Hellooooo."

The "said with" construction we looked at earlier also creates, as my granny used to say, a "bassackward" effect because it follows a line of dialogue. For example:

> "Ants," he said with fear in his voice.

The reader needs to be shown the fear, not told, before the speech:

> His eyes widened when black specks marched under the door, and his voice broke when he said, "Ants."

This gives the reader a chance of "hearing" the word "ants" with the speaker's abnormal delivery. A small point, perhaps, but a novel is made up of thousands of small points that either add up to the experience of the novel or just a compilation of information. For my money, you need to make every small point contribute to the experience.

Test your dialogue to see if:

- Your dialogue tags are either "said" or not there at all (well, maybe an occasional "shouted" or "whispered" is okay)

- You include internal monologue and action beats that characterize or move the story forward
- You show the dialogue happening instead of explaining it with "with"
- You clue the reader to the sound of a speech before it happens

Section 3: Story

TELLING A STORY SEEMS LIKE a simple enough proposition: you just set down what happens, right?

But to be a novelist or a memoirist that people pay to read, telling your tale can't be what you'd do settin' on the porch and jawing about what happened to Uncle Abner back in '98, no sirree. It has to be compelling. (On the other hand, if we're talking about how Uncle Abner single-handedly defeated the attack of the space aliens . . . hmmmm.)

What makes a story compelling? How do you make it compelling? This section takes up the story side of writing a novel or memoir, the thinking and planning and conceptualizing and imagining you have to do to reach a publishable level of story.

There are no magical answers, no one formula that you can input with characters and events that sums to a compelling story. This is an art, after all.

And there are no rules, either. If you do the opposite of everything advised in this book but in doing so you create the experience of a compelling story, that's great.

No rules, no magical answers . . . but there are ways to think about how to craft what happens that create tension in your story, the necessary ingredient that forces readers to turn pages.

Story as river

A TALE OF TWO STORIES:

Enticed by a friend's recommendation, Ima Reader takes a seat in a punt on the shore of a gentle English river. The flat-bottom boat rocks a little, but she feels safe in the hands of Heezan Author, who stands ready at the stern, hands on the long pole used to push the boat. His photo on the back of the book was nice.

Heezan shoves off, and they glide down the river on an easy-going current. Heezan says, "Note the lovely hues of red and gold in the rose garden on the far bank." He steers the bow a few degrees toward the near shore. "And here is the poor peasant hut, its thatched roof more holes than not, where our hero was born, poor tyke, the sad victim of—"

"Oh, the hero. I'm so eager to see him." Ima leans forward and peers ahead.

"Soon enough, soon enough, Dear Reader. But first, see the ramshackle one-room school-house where Hero first met Heroine, though their meeting was a tussle over who got the swing—"

Ima turns to Heezan. "Excuse me, sir . . ."

A sigh. "Yes?"

"Pull over to the bank, please."

"But there's so much story to be told."

The boat clunks against a dock and Ima steps out. "Too late." She gently closes the covers, never to return.

OR . . .

Feeling the pull of a fetching blurb, Ima Reader turns to page one and drops into a river raft. It races downstream, toward the roar of water churning over rocks. The raft noses around a bend, and ahead spray creates a mist above roiling water and granite boulders.

Sheezan Author, both hands with strangle-holds on the rudder at the rear, shouts, "I don't want to alarm you, but there are crocodiles between us and the end."

Ima grips a page. Her lips stretch in a grin of anticipation when she leans forward and says, "Let 'er rip!"

What if Ima Reader is an agent to whom you've just submitted a sample, and yours is the eleventy-eleventh submission she's opened that week?

Or an acquisitions editor at a publishing firm who wonders why in hell he agreed to look at your manuscript?

Or a bookstore browser deciding on what to buy for a weekend read? These people turn to page one looking for one thing.

To be swept away.

And effortlessly, too. After all, the agent's tired, it's been a hard week, she's looked at dozens of crappy novels, and it's an act of will to tackle another one. The editor feels a migraine coming on, and the bookstore browser just had her transmission go out. Please, capture my mind and imagination and take me away from all this.

But how does a story do that? The story river readers want to ride races down mountain slopes, hurtles around sharp bends to reveal unexpected events, plunges into canyons and out again until a killer waterfall comes into view. Then it sweeps them over, they plunge and crash into the maelstrom of the story's climax, and then emerge into calm waters, safe and satisfied.

But how does an author sweep a reader along? The reader isn't in a craft pulled by a rope, nor is it propelled by oars or a motor. Instead, her imagination becomes one with the flow of the river.

What determines the nature of that flow? What lack makes it an easy-going stream, what element makes it a roller-coaster ride?

For a river, gravity furnishes passive power with inevitable pull. Where does the power of a story come from?

The gap

Screenwriter/story guru Robert McKee has a terrific way of thinking about what powers a story. Years back, I attended one of his intensive seminars on screenwriting, and I wish now I'd been ready to understand everything he had to offer. A brilliant screenwriter and story thinker, McKee nails what creates the ever-increasing rush of current in a story's river. In his book, *Story*, he calls it the "gap," the thing that stymies the protagonist. While he writes primarily about screenwriting, he does talk about novels, and his insights are all about story, no matter what the form.

The following diagram from his book illustrates the gap.

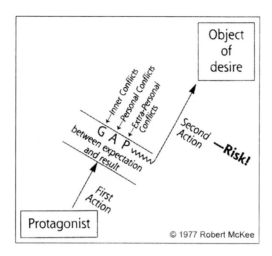

A character has an object of desire. That could be a treasure, a job, a person, catching a killer, anything. He takes action—risky action—to get it . . . but he doesn't succeed because of inner, personal, or external conflict—or a combination of conflicts. A gap opens between the character and his goal.

But he still wants what he wants—or, better, needs what he needs. So he takes a second action, one with greater risk. But again he is frustrated and must try again. McKee says each effort should involve more risk; each time there should be more for the character to lose. Causes of the gap can even be things that seem pleasant, even the achievement of a similar goal . . . but underneath, like the current in the river, there's still that need that isn't satisfied.

So look at your story, especially the opening. Are you poling your reader down a lazy river, talking amiably about scenery and backstory? Or about to run the rapids only seconds after your reader boards?

The rapids don't, of course, have to be physical as in an adventure story. They can be caused by internal conflict. They can be emotional, or interpersonal, or . . . hey, whatever your imagination desires.

A RIVER IS NOT ALL RAPIDS

Your story river needs the tension of rapids and crocodiles to keep compelling readers forward, but keep in mind that a river, just as a story, needs eddies and calm pools, too. Without them, the traveler can be exhausted. Without them, the story cannot gather its energy for another run. Moments of calm serve to create more tension if your story has let the reader know—through your use of the gap—that all is not yet well.

But your river must still MOVE! In *Gundown,* the protagonist goes to a peaceful seaside resort when he is freed from a terrible prison. Yet, nice as it all is, the story river's current is still beneath him (and the reader), and he soon goes back into action, recharged but still having a goal he must achieve.

When I write scenes and chapters, I don't consciously apply McKee's gap technique before writing. But my sense of that underlying mechanism is becoming more and more ingrained in me, more of the rudder that steers my characters deeper and deeper into complications.

USE THE GAP TO GIVE FIRST AID TO YOUR STORY

"The gap" can be a terrific diagnostic tool. If your story feels lazy or sags somewhere along the line, look at what is (and isn't) happening—does the character desire something, does he strive for it, is he blocked and forced to try again, to try something new at greater and greater risk?

Put "the gap" to work to help you create an irresistible pull for the river of your story.

Start with kitty-cats in action

IF YOU ARE STROLLING in your neighborhood and come upon the above scene in progress, I defy you to just keep going and not stop to see what happens next.

In the same way, opening your story in *media res,* in the midst of something happening versus placidly setting the scene, is key to engaging a reader. For example:

Hairball raced across the clover, leaping honeybees, never taking his gaze from Barfie, praying that her grip would hold.

This opening raises immediate story questions that a reader will want to know the answers to—why is Hairball racing? Who is Barfie? What is Barfie? What do they have to do with each other? What's Barfie's scary-sounding problem?

What if we add consequences or stakes to the action? Opening with action that confronts a character with a significant challenge that has serious consequences will move a reader down the page.

Hairball eyed the tree's towering height. It was an impossible climb. He was too small, too weak. But if he didn't climb, Barfie would fall to her death.

Now let's combine action with jeopardy for increased tension.

Barfie dug her claws into the branch, struggling to keep her balance. She dared not look down; her last glance at the dizzying height had almost sent her tumbling. Her ears caught a cracking sound . . . the branch was tearing away from the trunk.

Yeeks! Now add conflict to action and jeopardy:

Hairball arched his back and hissed at the beast. It was three times his size, an alien species that crouched, poised to spring. There was no place to run. He extended his claws and braced himself.

Not all openings have to begin with physical action . . . but they MUST begin to raise story questions immediately. Remember that thoughts are action, too. Next we open with a character facing a different sort of jeopardy.

Hairball wondered if Barfie's spirit now rested on one of the puffy pillows in the sky, freed from her broken body. How would he face her mother after he'd sworn she would be safe?

Approaches you can use to kick-start your novel include:

- Start with something happening.
- Open with action that challenges the character.
- Combine action with jeopardy for the character.
- Add conflict to action and jeopardy.

The point of all this is that your opening page narrative has to first be vivid enough to catch the reader's thoughts and then compel reading further by raising story questions. For a new writer to break in, the opening page of every chapter ought to do the same thing.

Well, hell, every page, right?

Tension in your first sentence

THERE'S A REASON for working to create tension with your very first sentence—it leads to the second sentence. You draw your reader into your story sentence by sentence by sentence. It's clear that each sentence on the first page is charged with the responsibility to KEEP READERS MOVING FORWARD.

Donald Maass, in *Writing the Breakout Novel:*

> "There is, in any great opening line, a miniconflict or tension that is strong enough to carry the reader to the next step of the narrative."

Jim Hess, a writing contest judge, says,

> "If you don't hook my attention and hold it in the first twenty-five to fifty words, you probably won't."

When you send a sample to an agent, or when an editor turns to your first page, or when a bookstore shopper picks your book up, you are on trial. Not just your work, but your ability. The agent/editor wants to know, can this writer engage me? Can this writer use language to make me read his story?

The story is on trial as well. You get a few hundred words to make your initial case that the journey through the next 85,000 words is worth it and that it will reward your reader with a helluva reading experience.

And it all starts with that first line.

But there are so many things in your mind when you craft that first sentence—setting the scene, characterizing, creating action, whatever—it's entirely possible to miss seeing a lack of tension.

Take me, for example. I had reworked the following first sentence scores of times, and it had evolved to this:

> As I approach the steps to the Chicago Art Institute, a lean man in a black overcoat sees me and then aims a video camera my way.

While it did what I wanted it to in many ways, including setting the scene and starting with action, it nagged at me that something was missing.

TENSION.

I realized that the problem—and the solution—lay in the verbs. While "sees" and "aimed" are descriptive enough and give you a clear picture of the man's movement, they are otherwise limp. They describe the action but don't characterize it in ways that can create tension.

I needed to add flavors that suggested something was amiss, that there might be jeopardy for the character. I didn't want to be as "on the nose" as something like "threatened." That wouldn't make a lot of sense this early in the story and would be ham-handed as well. I think the replacement verbs I used do the trick:

> As I approach the steps to the Chicago Art Institute, a lean man in a black overcoat eyes me and then targets me with a video camera.

I think "eyes me" adds subtle motive and intent that "sees me" just doesn't have, and "targets" adds an element of purpose to the man's action and the emotional overtones the protagonist feels. And what do we do with targets? We hit them or shoot at them. That, it seems to me, is implicit in this choice of verb; my protagonist, Annie, feels like a target, and that adds tension.

In addition, since we're in Annie's deep point of view, this adds to characterization because it's her interpretation of a normally innocent action that lets the reader know that, for some reason, she sees it as a threat.

This is a tiny bit of writing for effect, true, but it contributes to the aggregate that delivers her experience.

After finding this soft spot in my own work, I decided to go through samples writers had sent and see how their first sentences fared in terms of creating some sense of tension. For example:

> In the moment after midnight, the world held
> its breath.

For me, lots of tension there. Why did the world hold its breath? Why at midnight? What's happening? Story questions! Here's another.

> There's something there.

I like that one, too. There's menace in those three words, and I want to know more. A bit of dialogue opened the next sample.

> "They're belly beads."

Hmm. Kinda interesting, but no hint of tension. In looking at the rest of the sample, there was no tension in the opening paragraphs. This writer will have to dig deeper.

Next, from *Nectar from a Stone,* by Jane Guill.

> Maelgwyn's "husbandly attention," as he called
> it, went on and on.

That opening line is packed with information and, for me, tension as well. In those eleven words I get the idea that sex is happening; that the recipient of Maelgwyn's attention doesn't think of it the same way that he does; and that she doesn't like it. This opening both establishes a relationship and smacks of the tension in it.

Here's another from a published work, E.B. White's *Charlotte's Web.*

> "Where's Papa going with that ax?"

I defy anyone to not rush to the next sentence. Now back to some of the samples sent to me by unpublished writers.

> Allison could sense something was wrong all
> the way to the roots of her fur.

There's tension alluded to here, but it doesn't grab me. I think it's the fact that I'm being told about the tension ("something was wrong") rather than being shown. Having her sense things is a form of "filtering," too. I took another part of the writer's opening paragraph and added it in this way:

> Allison's father stepped into the doorway, and
> she tensed all the way to the roots of her fur.

That's a start at raising story questions and writing for effect. What about this one?

> Inspector Steve Masters of the National Security
> Branch watched her stride down the airport
> concourse.

Only the man's title and the "Security Branch" hint at tension, and vaguely. The lack lies in the action—just watching someone isn't tension-provoking. How about just a couple of tweaks . . .

> Inspector Steve Masters of the National Security
> Branch tracked his quarry through the airport
> concourse.

Just changing the action from watching to tracking and "her" to being his quarry did wonders for the tension. Another example:

> Grace stirred in bed, kept her eyes closed.

Nope. But a few sentences later, the writer had this:

> A floorboard creaked beneath the worn carpet.

Now, if that had been the first sentence, and then we had Grace stirring but keeping her eyes closed, I would wonder what Grace isn't seeing that makes the floor creak—there would be tension afoot.

> A floorboard creaked beneath the worn carpet.
> Grace stirred in her bed, kept her eyes closed.

Next:

> Boccaha was a small fat balding man with bad
> teeth.

That simple description caused no tightening in my mind. For one thing, he's not doing anything, as far as we can see. As it happened in this sample, it took a couple of hundred words of exposition before anything actually happened.

Here's an opening (very long) sentence that focuses on scene.

> A crisp, bitter winter wind knifed between the buildings of downtown Seattle, slashing like transparent rapids through the alleys and streets, seeping into the cracks around doors and windows, and stealing under people's coats and hats as nature sought to balance hot and cold.

While I applaud the writer's effort to set the scene, and he has used active verbs, all we're really seeing is a windy day. No tension here. As it happened, his second paragraph started this way:

> Darren McAllister's stiffening body lay face-up in a green, rusted metal Dumpster, half-hidden by discarded pizza boxes and a bulging black plastic trash bag.

Okay, now you've got me. Add the wind in later, if you must, but give me tension to begin with. Writers often have a real grabber of an opening sentence that comes later in the narrative.

Here's a writer who didn't wait around.

> She couldn't run any more, but she didn't dare stop.

Applause, applause. I want more. Guaranteed that I'll move on to the next sentence, and the writer increases her chances of hooking me. How about this one?

The Reverend David Wilcox was walking slowly
across the wet grass towards the rectory, where
his friend Dr. Alex Greer was waiting for him.

No sale. This was from a murder mystery. Not even enhancing the verbs ("walking slowly" needs help) would add edge to this simple movement. But about 1,200 words later in the story was this sentence:

He lowered the pillow over Emily's face and
pressed down firmly.

Now we're talking.

Go to the first line on your first page. If there's no tension, look for a way to add it—there's an agent or editor waiting to drop the blade like an executioner if he's not lured further into the story.

Six vital story ingredients

WHAT ARE THE ELEMENTS that make up a compelling narrative? What can you use to propel a reader onward? You can make sure your narrative has as many of these story elements as possible:

- Story questions
- Tension (in the reader)
- Voice
- Scene-setting
- Character
- Clarity

There are more elements to a story, of course, and adequate grammar is a prerequisite, but these six are critical tools for engaging a reader, factors that can create the hook you need to reel in a weary agent or browsing reader.

STORY QUESTIONS

My list starts with story questions because without them there would be zero tension. Story questions are created and raised by what is happening in the NOW of the story and need to be strong enough to force a reader to read on. They are primarily "what happens next" questions. They are plot questions.

- Will he get out of the trap?
- Will she be shot by the killer?

- Will the giant spider eat them?

An example that immediately raises a story question:

> When he grasped Sheila's throat, she bared her
> teeth, grabbed his shirt with one hand, and drew
> back her fist.

The story questions are: Will she hit him? Will he free himself? Will he hurt her? What happens next? This is the kind of story question that keeps a reader reading.

But there are questions that should not be raised: ***information questions.*** They are about something the reader can't know. I have seen opening pages that had statements like this one:

> Only Simone could have known what he did.

That would be okay if the narrative had let the reader know who Simone was and what the unnamed he had done. Unfortunately, it hadn't.

Here's another example, an opening paragraph:

> When they learn what has happened, the truth
> of it will own them. They will be completely
> overtaken by the raw reality of it. In that mo-
> ment, everything else in the universe will become
> invisible to them.

In this case, the reader did not know who "they" was, nor what happened, nor the truth of it. The entire paragraph is fundamentally meaningless. Other examples:

- Reference to an unknown creature that hasn't been mentioned: Raising his weapon, he blasted the articulated bandersnatch.

- Reference to an organization that hasn't been mentioned: The president vowed to stop the attack by S.N.A.R.P.
- Reference to an event that hasn't been mentioned by a person who hasn't been mentioned: Norman basked in the glow of his victory.

Withholding information from the reader to create a question does not increase tension, it can actually decrease tension and take a reader out of the story.

Back to story questions—here's an example of building tension with story questions that are asked and answered. How about this for the very first sentence you encounter in a novel?

The spider crept onto Judy's bare neck.

Your knowledge of spiders raises instant questions: Will it bite Judy? Is it poisonous? Is it deadly? What will happen if she's bitten? Will she feel the spider and avoid the bite? What's going to happen next?!

Let's add a little more information and see what happens to the story questions.

 The black widow spider crept onto Judy's bare neck.

Uh-oh. Now you know it's poisonous, and its bite has more serious consequences—the stakes have been raised, the story question is intensified, and the tension mounts. The higher the stakes, the greater the possibility that harm or trouble will come to the character, the stronger the story question.

Now you also "see" the spider more clearly—it's black! Is that enough tension? Enough story questions? Can we make things worse for Judy?

Yep.

The black widow spider crept onto Judy's bare
neck. She stirred in her sleep.

She's asleep? Ohmygod! New story question: will she wake
up in time to deal with the spider? Once more:

 The black widow spider crept onto
Judy's bare neck. She stirred in her
sleep. A second black widow crawled
onto her naked skin.

New story questions (and tension): How many black widows
are there? Where is she that there are so many? The stakes are
higher than ever. What will happen next?! Is she going to wake
up? And we did this with only three sentences. Just for fun, what
if this comes next?

Judy opened her eyes just as the first spider
crawled onto her cheek.

Story question answered: she's awake! Now she can deal with
the threat, but there are new questions: what will she do and will
she escape? Here's what happens next:

She looked down to see what tickled, and then
she grinned.

How's that for a story-question-raiser?

Two kinds of story questions

Judy's grin in the last sentence of the spider example
brings up a second kind of story question. Rather than asking "what happens next?" it asks "why did that happen?"

While you see the "why" question less frequently than "what," it comes from character and can lead to an expansion and deepening of character that further engages the reader.

TENSION

In discussions of writing craft, you hear about "tension" all the time. But what does that mean? Is it conflict on every page? Not necessarily. It means something in your narrative that creates a need in your reader, a small unease, a hunger to know more. It means that what happens in the story causes tension in the reader and fosters the lure of what will happen next. Tension is a real feeling that you, the reader, should experience on the first page of a novel. We're not saying break-out-in-a-sweat tension here, more like an itch-that-has-to-be-scratched version.

We're not talking about tension in the character, either. A character might be scared to death, but unless we care about that character, it won't matter. Heck, a character can be relaxed and happy, or asleep like Judy with the spiders was. The tension created in that little episode was in you, the reader.

As for conflict, it can be a good thing to have on the first page, but you don't have to have the main conflict there to create tension. While it might be a stronger hook to begin with something like this . . .

> In ten seconds, the dirty bomb would contaminate Manhattan with enough radiation to make it a desert for fifty centuries.

. . . the tension element, as long as it comes from story questions that are meaningful to the reader, can be relatively mild compared to the overall conflict or jeopardy in the story. For example, the opening sentence from *Fly by Night* by Frances Hardinge:

"But names are important!" the nursemaid
protested.

By definition a protest is conflict, and story questions come
tumbling out of this first sentence, certainly enough to carry you
to the next sentence, and thus giving the writer a chance to sink
her claws in deeper.

But immediate conflict isn't the only way to create tension,
although it's hard to beat as a hook-setter. Jeopardy, a sense of
trouble ahead, can create plenty of tension to move the reader
just enough further for more of the story to take hold. Here's the
opening sentence from one of my novels, *The Vampire Kitty-cat
Chronicles:*

Just after dark, death grabbed me by the tail.

VOICE

What the heck is "voice?" Here's a definition adapted from
Self-editing for Fiction Writers: "it is the way sentences read as
prose." I will add this: it is how they sound in your head.

Literary agent Andrea Somberg defines it this way:

". . . a writing style that pulls me in and makes
me feel like I'm a part of the story and the characters' lives."

In fiction, there are two basic voices: that of the author and
that of a character. In this book, the voice you read/hear is mine. I
can cut loose and do what I want, unrestricted by theme or venue
or a character. I'm the character.

In fiction written from the omniscient point of view, the
voice is the author's. When well done, as with authors such as
John Irving, an author's voice can succeed in engaging the reader.

Here's the opening from Irving's *The Fourth Hand:*

> Imagine a young man on his way to a less-than-thirty-second event—the loss of his left hand, long before he reached middle age.
>
> As a schoolboy, he was a promising student, a fair-minded and likable kid, without being terribly original. Those classmates who could remember the future hand recipient from his elementary-school days would never have described him as daring. Later, in high school, his success with girls notwithstanding, he was rarely a bold boy, certainly not a reckless one. While he was irrefutably good-looking, what his former girlfriends would recall as most appealing about him was that he deferred to them.

The other voices you hear in fiction are those of the characters. When you're using a deep third person POV, that includes description of action and setting within a particular character's narrative. The writer suppresses his own voice and brings out that of the character. I frequently see instances where a narrative that's supposed to be that of a child is robbed of authenticity by word choices in the descriptive elements that are clearly adult in nature.

To exemplify, here's how the narratives of three very different characters describe the same incident, falling off a bicycle:

A SEVEN-YEAR-OLD BOY:

> The front wheel hit a rock and he fell and hit the ground hard. He skinned his knee and it bled a lot. His mom was gonna be mad about the rip in his pants.

A TEENAGE BOY:

The front wheel banged into a big freakin' rock and the handlebars ripped out of his hands. He flew off the bike and crashed. The pavement trashed his jeans and skinned his knee, which bled like a stuck pig. It hurt like hell, and Jenny wasn't going to want to go to the movie with him looking like this.

A MIDDLE-AGED COLLEGE PROFESSOR:

The front wheel struck a large rock and the handlebars twisted from his grasp. He plunged over the falling bicycle and slammed into the asphalt road. The black, gritty surface tore open his jeans and scraped skin from his kneecap. It bled furiously and he cursed the rock, hoping he hadn't fractured the knee.

I've read that a number of agents profess that voice is sometimes the thing they respond to most in a submission. Back to agent Andrea Somberg:

"Every manuscript I take on is distinctive in its own right, but each of them has one thing in common: an engaging narrative voice."

Voice is the one thing that can suck you into a story even without initial tension and story questions (though those requirements cannot be avoided for long, and it's certainly better to have them than not).

Perhaps it's easier to think about what voice does rather than what it is. Here are some characteristics of a voice that will lead a reader on:

Freshness. It "sounds" fresh in the reader's mind. The language is not mundane, but has flavor. The ideas evoked are out of the ordinary. The way things are put is uncommon. Words that create a distinct sense of "personality" is another way to think of this aspect of voice. A first-person narrative should generate a fresh-sounding voice.

Confidence. A strong voice immediately says to a reader, "You can trust me. I know a terrific story, and you can relax and enjoy because I know how to tell it so well that it becomes an experience in your mind." Stephen King's voice has that confidence.

Lucidity. A clear voice that slips scenes and sights and sounds easily into your mind, with no struggle to comprehend or follow, can sweep you swiftly into the current of a story.

By the way, as an editor I work hard to respect and preserve a writer's voice. It would be too easy to rewrite so that it "sounds" better to me because it sounds *like* me. You may see examples in this book where you don't care for the voice all that much. Me neither, but the writer has to have a chance to try it out.

CLARITY

Maybe the need for this story element on your first page seems obvious, but it can be harder to achieve than you think. Take this opening sentence from one of my workshoppers:

> Mark Johnson's daughter had disappeared, and that was all that mattered to him.

What could have been an intriguing opening was, for me, diminished by what it fails to make clear: What is the relationship between the missing girl and the point-of-view character, the "him?" Is she Mark Johnson's daughter or is she someone else's?

Because the pronoun "him" in first sentence is unclear as to whom it refers, the disappearing daughter could be an as-yet-unnamed protagonist's, or that of a friend, or boss, or a crime victim. Yes, we know that the girl matters to "him," and we might assume that she's his daughter, but it isn't clear.

If you simply reverse the positions of the pronoun and the name, the clarity issue is solved.

> His daughter had disappeared, and that was all
> that mattered to Mark Johnson.

Readers want reading your story to be effortless, as well—they should be able to absorb and react without having to stop and think about the stimuli you put on a piece of paper. That is not to say that good storytelling doesn't give you something to think about—it should. Clear meaning is the critical hurdle your writing must clear.

Here's another example; this description is from the point of view of someone inside an airplane.

> In the distance, the ice-capped peaks of the
> Rockies rose intermittently among the clouds.
> Far above the peaks, the roar of the airplane
> pierced the shrieking winds of the atmosphere.

The dissonance here, for me, was that in the first sentence the peaks are in the distance and in the second the airplane is above them. Isn't the following more clear?

> The ice-capped peaks of the Rockies rose inter-
> mittently among the clouds. High above them,
> the roar of the airplane pierced the shrieking
> winds of the atmosphere.

SCENE-SETTING

One of the most damaging flaws I see in manuscripts is failure to set the scene effectively—or at all. Some read more like radio scripts than novels. Others are simply underdone, probably because the writer puts down a sparse description that evokes the whole picture in his mind but fails to get it in on paper. Why is that a problem? Primarily because, although readers bring their imaginations to your novel and willingly take part in fleshing out the vision, they need to experience characters and action in context. It helps a reader to slip into the shoes of a character if she knows whether the shoes are walking along a snow-covered sidewalk or wading a jungle stream.

I'll illustrate. First, a snippet of dialogue.

> Roger said, "Don't you think that's a bit skimpy?"
>
> Maggie twirled. "You don't like it?"

Context can give meaning. I'll put these players into two different contexts to show how the meaning of their dialogue is affected.

> Roger opened the dressing room door and found Maggie admiring herself in a full-length mirror. He stepped inside and shut the door on the caterwauling of the woman currently on stage. Even though Maggie was the next to perform, she didn't seem nervous at all. Roger said, "Don't you think that's a bit skimpy?"
>
> Maggie twirled. "You don't like it?"

Okay, now let's use the same dialogue but put it into a different context.

> The window rattled with the impact of the Arctic Express that had struck the city that morning. Roger pulled on his parka and then scraped frost off the glass to peer into the swirling snow outside. He turned to find Maggie waiting at the front door. Roger said, "Don't you think that's a bit skimpy?"
>
> Maggie twirled. "You don't like it?"

We don't yet know what Maggie is wearing, but we do know that in the first situation Roger doesn't think she should go out in front of an audience with that little on. In this context, the subtext is that Roger is possessive and jealous, and his concern is about losing Maggie because she's so attractive to others.

In the second example, he doesn't think she's sufficiently protected against a dangerous storm. The context leads us to think of Roger as a caring man who is concerned about Maggie's well-being.

In each case, where the scene is set and how the environment in which these characters act impacts them create context and give meaning to the character's actions and words. Context can effortlessly give the reader an understanding—even better, a feeling—for what's happening. And in these examples, context tells us that conflict is just about to blossom.

Ahhh, tension.

Please, set the scene early on, within the context of action, so that when you get to what's happening the reader knows where it happens. And keep in mind that it can be brief—the two examples above set the scene sufficiently with just two sentences.

CHARACTER

While plot is a tool to engage and entertain a reader, it is character that makes them come to care about what happens, it is character that invests meaning into what happens and, in fact, it is character that creates plot by the decisions made.

Take every chance you have to add to the characterization of your protagonist—or antagonist—to more deeply engage your reader. And that requires action.

You know the old saw, "Do as I say, not as I do." Well, it's the reverse of this cliché that applies in fiction and memoir—character derives from action, not words. If a politician says he wants an honorable campaign that focuses on issues yet he directs his campaign to spew slur after slur at his opponent, then which is the true reflection of the politician's character?

A character's words can lie, too. Fiction sometimes uses the literary device of an "unreliable narrator" in which the credibility of the teller of the story is compromised. The character of an unreliable narrator comes from both what he does and the contrast with what he says. Behavior (action) is character.

More than that, the events of a story—plot—should spring from what a character does, not simply be things that happen to him. It is what a character decides to do that should create events. For example, let's consider this boy at a new school.

> Ron strolled past the gym at recess. It was his first day in seventh grade, and he didn't know anyone at this school. He hated moving.
>
> But there had been a nice moment in English class. The teacher had just started when a girl rushed in right after the bell. She looked for a place to sit, but all the desks were taken.
>
> He didn't know why, but he had stood, picked up his books, and gestured her to his seat.
>
> The smile she had given him—and she was a super pretty girl—had just about wiped out what the teacher had said for the rest of the class.

A deep voice came from his left. "Hey, goody two-shoes."

Three boys lounged on a porch at the side of the gym. The big one looked like a man. He even had a mustache. That one said, "Why'd you give Carol your seat?" The "goody two-shoes" had come from him.

Ron shrugged.

The big kid swaggered over to Ron and scowled down. "We don't do that chickenshit stuff here."

Ron had to look up; God, the boy was big. Fighting words. Coming from a monster.

Ron's first choice of action, giving up his seat in the classroom, revealed a facet of character, and has led to a plot development, conflict with a really big, nasty guy. Ron's next action will reveal character at a deeper level. If he keeps his mouth shut, or maybe even runs, he's a coward. In this case, here's what Ron did:

Ron gazed straight into the boy/man's eyes and said, "Well, where I come from, it's what a gentleman does." Then he had to look away. He stepped around the big guy and walked, every muscle in his back tensed.

Now new story (plot) questions are raised as a result of Ron's decision to say what he said and then turn away. Will the big guy come after him? Will Ron get away with this? What will happen next is determined by what he does.

Mastering the first page

As agent Lori Perkins said,

> "Your novel has to grab me by the first page, which is why I can reject you on page one."

Well, here's a first-page checklist to help you past that hurdle:

A First-Page Checklist:

- It begins *connecting the reader with the protagonist.*
- *Something is happening.* This does NOT include a character musing about whatever.
- *What happens is dramatized* in an immediate scene with action and description plus, if it works, dialogue.
- What happens *moves the story forward.*
- What happens *has consequences* for the protagonist.
- The protagonist *desires something.*
- The protagonist *does something.*
- *There's enough of a setting* to orient the reader as to where things are happening.
- It *happens in the NOW* of the story.
- *Backstory? What backstory?* We're in the NOW of the story.

- *Set-up? What set-up?* We're in the NOW of the story.
- What happens *raises a story question*—what happens next? or why did that happen?

You know what? This is also the next-page checklist.

In fact, it's the every-page checklist.

True, later in a novel there are exceptions to be made regarding backstory, flashbacks, and set-up, but if this checklist is your guide you will be reminded to keep those elements to the minimum necessary, to intrude on the story the least.

An average manuscript page (double-spaced, 12-point type, one-inch margins) is between 200 and 250 words long, and the beginnings of chapters even shorter—so you shouldn't feel compelled to cram every element of the checklist into every page. But you can put every page to the checklist test, which could help you identify places where the narrative lags or you've strayed from the story's true path.

A caveat:

On the other hand, it is entirely possible to craft a compelling first page, especially in a first-person narrative, without meeting all of the guidelines. I turned the page in one of the examples in the Workouts section even though the writer didn't do these things:

- ~~Something is happening. This does NOT include a character musing about whatever.~~
- ~~What happens is dramatized in an immediate scene with action and description plus, if it works, dialogue.~~
- ~~The protagonist does something.~~
- ~~It happens in the NOW of the story.~~
- ~~Backstory? What backstory? We're in the NOW of the story.~~
- ~~Set-up? What set-up? We're in the NOW of the story.~~

Whatever works.

The inciting incident: story launch pad

EVERY GOOD STORY IS launched by an "inciting incident." But does it have to be on page one? In surfing the Internet I came across advice in one place to make it happen at the opening of your story and in another place to have it occur as soon as possible after the story opens. I think that's mostly right, but not altogether. First, just exactly what is an inciting incident?

Robert McKee defines it this way in *Story:*

> An event that radically upsets the balance of forces in the protagonist's life.

So when must the inciting event occur? Well, there's no imbalance created unless the reader has some idea of the life the protagonist currently knows. If you can find a way to make it happen within a paragraph or two of the opening of your story, I think that's a smart thing to do. However, it can happen later— but only if there are other story questions that propel the reader along the stream of your narrative.

McKee cites the film *Rocky* as an example of a delayed inciting incident. He says the true inciting event is where Rocky is invited to fight the world champion. But that doesn't happen until a half hour into the film. Until then, the story that keeps the audience involved is the developing love story between Rocky and Adrian.

Wherever the inciting incident occurs, what precedes it must have tension, must be raising story questions that keep the reader involved. It can't just be exposition that lays out the protagonist's life.

A question rises in me from McKee's definition: How much does a reader first have to understand about the protagonist's life to give the imbalance meaning? I often see manuscripts in which the effort to do this leads to gobs of exposition that stop the story cold. To complicate matters, consummate professional Kurt Vonnegut says that you should give the reader a lot of information first (I disagree). In *Rocky*, the film takes a long time to first create Rocky's life. But keep in mind that a theater audience is a captive audience and that the romance raises story questions.

The answer lies in the nature of the incident. For a crime victim who is stabbed or shot, the imbalance is immediate and clear. In a literary novel, it might be much more subtle.

Now that I think about it, I wonder if Rocky meeting Adrian isn't the real inciting incident—would he have accepted the fight challenge if he and his life hadn't already been substantially changed by falling in love? I think not.

Another way to look at understanding the inciting incident is to key in on the word "provoke."

> An event that provokes a desire in the protagonist
> that he is compelled to satisfy.

"Compelled" is the key. If he can say forget about it, it's not much of a desire, is it? Here's another one:

> An event that forces a character to take action
> in pursuit of something he needs.

McKee would argue that a protagonist's desire is to bring her life back into balance. That makes sense to me, but it seems too abstract. Specifically, what is the nature of this incident?

It can be negative (and, it seems, usually is).

- The banker's children are kidnapped.
- An innocent woman is accused of a hideous crime.
- A single mother is fired from her job.

The event can be positive, too, but so hugely positive that it can throw a life out of balance and create new desires.

- Rocky is invited to fight the champ.
- A grocery clerk wins the lottery.
- A secretary is promoted over her boss.
- A battered woman escapes to a shelter.
- A man in a happy relationship is smitten by a beautiful woman.

I think McKee's notion that the inciting event throws a protagonist's life out of balance is a good one. Anything out of balance is bound to create tension and conflict—will it fall? Will it right itself? The main result of the event, to create a desire in the character to regain balance, is the fuel that fires the engine of your story.

In McKee's scheme of things, your protagonist must have a powerful desire. He must then attempt to satisfy it. But his attempt is frustrated. He fails to achieve it because of something the antagonist does (preferably), or perhaps something the protagonist fails to do, or some other story element.

Your story picks up momentum and tension at this point because the character has to try again and, because of the nature of his failure and his desire, has to take a risk. A risk with negative consequences. Yep, he fails again. The negative consequences raise the stakes. He has to try again, and this time take an even greater risk. With greater consequences. He fails again. And so on.

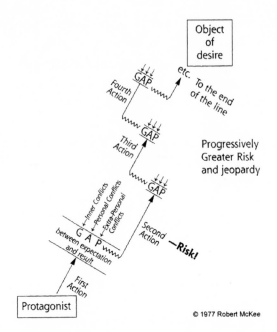

© 1977 Robert McKee

For example, in a historical novel, let's say the daughter of a king is sent to live with the neighboring king in the age-old tradition of fostering. This upsets the balance of her happy life at home and she may have a desire to stay there, but the consequences are potentially positive, and she makes no effort to change things. This isn't an inciting incident because, even though the balance of her life is disturbed, there's no jeopardy attached.

Then, on the journey to the neighboring kingdom, her party is attacked. She is taken and sold as a slave to another kingdom. Now that's an inciting incident. Her desire is to return to the life she knew, and there's the risk of being beaten, raped, or killed if she tries to escape. But try she must, because her life as a slave is a horror to her. You can write the story from there.

An engine named desire

WE TALKED ABOUT DESIRE as an element of the inciting incident, and Robert McKee points to it in his gap theory. But desire isn't just for the inciting incident. Here's Rick DeMarinis, *The Art & Craft of the Short Story:*

> "Fiction is about trouble. Trouble is a direct consequence of desire. Characters are living embodiments of desire. A character in need is the force that sets a story in motion."

I was watching a Winter Olympics race when an American speed skater was knocked down by a competitor who fell. The American slid blades-first into the side barrier, on her back, clearly out of the race.

But even before she'd stopped slamming into the barrier she was scrambling to regain her feet. The instant she was up-right her entire focus went down the ice. The intensity in her eyes and the set of her mouth were almost palpable, even on a television screen.

She took off, her desire still powerful, her determination everything, and my heart and admiration went out to her. I was rooting for her. And respecting her. And liking her.

If you can get a reader feeling that way about your character, you're on the way to compelling storytelling. So how do you do that?

CREATE DESIRE.

Robert McKee says that a story's inciting incident is an event that radically upsets the balance of forces in the character's life. But to what end?

He goes on to say that the character must react to the event, otherwise there would be no story. But react with what?

A desire. A goal to be achieved. The high-octane fuel that gives your story power.

In McKee's approach, the desire is for the character to put his/her life back into balance. Let's say a character's children are kidnapped. Of course the character doesn't think, "Dang, my life is out of balance. My desire is to regain my balance." No, the desire would be a specific goal, to get his children back from the kidnappers.

Is this right, then? A desire? Another writing instruction book tells us that fiction is about trouble. And we've all heard the cliché: get your character up a tree and throw rocks at him until he figures out how to get down.

But is the "trouble" model passive, where characters just react and react and react? Dodge a rock, dodge a rock, dodge a rock?

An initial "trouble" may be the cause—the inciting incident—of the character's first desire, but further trouble needs to come *because of what characters do*, to happen as a result of the risks they take to achieve their desire.

It's this pursuit of a desire that creates the "rooting factor" that draws readers into a story, that gives them something to identify and empathize with. Just as I did that Olympic skater.

The "strive" is the thing. One of my editing clients was a good writer. He'd done his research well, the language was good. He'd created a pleasant, likeable character. Smart. Pretty. Decent.

But the character just drifted through her life, reacting to things, never initiating much, not striving. There was no tension.

Nothing compelling me to turn the page. My recommendation was to create a strong inciting incident at the front of the story, to knock the character far out of her happy life.

Why isn't a happy story good enough? Why is it a good idea to trouble our characters, knock them down, and then keep knocking them down as they struggle? Why does that make them more compelling, more watchable?

Because, as human beings, we struggle too. In our ordinary lives, we may struggle with things small or large, but struggle we must. We understand how a character who has been knocked down feels. And here's the thing that a novel can do that lifts it from being mere entertainment: show us something about how to be a human being.

Learning to be a human being has a lifelong learning curve, and we can use all the help we can get because there aren't many good instruction books. Although novels are fiction, they can instruct us on the truths of being human. So can memoirs.

Fiction models behavior for us, teaches us what (in the writer's imagination) works and what doesn't work. We like to see characters desire and yearn and attempt and fail and attempt again because it helps us understand, maybe, what we can do in our own lives.

In thinking about my first novel after coming across McKee's idea of creating a desire in a character, I thought I'd failed to do that in my main protagonist: it seemed to me that he mostly reacted to events.

But then I realized that, unwittingly, I'd done one of the things McKee talks about: created an unconscious desire. My character's inciting event really pulled the rug out from under his life, but on the surface he seemed satisfied with the way things were. He just wanted, it seemed, to keep on doing his work. But unconsciously, it was the opposite.

My job as a writer is to learn to do it wittingly.

McKee says that a story is more powerful if a character has an unconscious desire that works in opposition to the conscious desire.

This is heady stuff for a simple guy like me, but I think I see how it can work. For example, let's say a man's wife is kidnapped and a ransom is demanded. His surface desire is to rescue her. That's what society, his friends, his peers, and he himself expects. Standard thriller stuff, you've seen it a thousand times.

But what if he hates his wife for a good reason? Then his unconscious desire, the one that can't be admitted out loud, is to somehow lose her. This may remind you of the plot of the film *Ruthless People,* only Danny DeVito's desire to get rid of Bette Midler, his wife, is far from unconscious.

In my novel, darned if my protagonist's unconscious desire didn't affect what happened when he pursued conscious goals. Eventually his conscious goal came to be the same as the unconscious one, and he grew when he achieved it.

CHECKLIST FOR YOUR NARRATIVE:
- Does it contain an inciting incident that throws your protagonist's life severely out of balance?
- Does your antagonist have an inciting incident, too, the thing that drives him to make an evil decision and take action?
- Does the event create a conscious desire in your character?
- Does your reader know about it?
- Does your character immediately take action, take a risk to achieve a goal that springs from the inciting event?
- Optional: is there an unconscious, contrary desire?

These are the elements that not only create the engine that will drive your story, they create the fuel. The horsepower of that engine, and its power to affect the reader, depend on:

- How severely your character's life is thrown for a loop, i.e., how damaging are the consequences, how high the stakes?
- The difficulty of achieving the desire that is aroused
- The size of the risks she must take to recover

Five ways to create tension

WE ALL HAVE PLENTY OF TENSION in our lives, so why on earth would we ask—no, *demand* more? Because it feels good in a page-turner story. What happens when you don't deliver a simmering dollop of tension on virtually every page of your novel manuscript?

- The agent mails a rejection.
- The acquisitions editor says, "Pass."
- The bookstore browser moves on.

Agents and editors all want to discover an outstanding story. They want to be compelled to turn your pages. But they see so many hundreds of submissions that your storytelling needs to be almost perfectly irresistible to get them to go much beyond page one. A reader has a lifetime of making decisions about first pages, and they definitely discriminate.

Tension doesn't have to come from bloody, balls-to-the-wall action; it can be torment inside a character's head, or a verbal duel in a courtroom, or receiving a diagnosis in a doctor's office.

Nor does it have to come entirely from the main conflict in your story. Donald Maass talks about using *bridging conflict* when you're not focused on the main pain. It's smaller conflict before the inciting incident event that launches the plot comes along, and it must be meaningful and intriguing. Ideally, it would be related to what the story is about. An example of bridging conflict:

Hamilton pulled his pillow over his head to shut out the pounding on the front door—it had been a late night celebrating getting a callback for that bacon commercial, although pitching bacon was a little creepy when he considered his porcine nature—

The pounding stopped. Good. Even muffled, he'd never get back to sleep with that racket going on.

Damn, now a voice screamed. Through the pillow filter it sounded like it said, "Mmmph smumm artak blisker!" He took the pillow off his head. The voice came in loud and clear.

"Pay your rent now or you're outta there now!"

He'd liked what it said better with the pillow over his head.

The voice shrieked, "Now! Now! Now! Now!"

How could he pacify his enraged landlord, especially since he was fresh out of cash after springing for champagne and truffles last night? It wouldn't be good to be a homeless actor in Hollywood. Or anywhere, for that matter. Maybe running away to pay another day would be best.

He headed for the back door, but pounding started there. It was different this time, though— more like a hammer on nails than a fist on a door.

He peeked through the café curtain over the window in the door and there hammered a scowling clown holding nails in his teeth.

The clown stopped hammering and peered in. His eyes widened and he spat nails.

Busted. Hamilton scurried for the front door.

The immediate conflict over the rent that's due provides action and interest that will, the writer hopes, take you to the later introduction of the primary conflict in the story.

CONTINUOUS MICRO-TENSION

Thriller writer Tess Gerritsen wrote in her blog about hearing a talk by Donald Maass on his notion of "continuous micro-tension." In a story with a high level of conflict, she says, there's ". . . an underlying sense that something important is always about to happen, or could happen."

Tess added her take on the technique.

> "Micro-tension is that sense that, on every page of the novel, there's conflict in the air, or that characters are slightly off-balance. It needn't be a flat-out argument or a gun battle or a huge confrontation. In fact, you can't throw in too many major conflicts or what you'll get is melodrama. But small and continuous doses of tension keep the story moving and keep the pages turning."

FRUSTRATE YOUR CHARACTER

In a critique group member's novel, she created a simple but effective bit of tension during a question-and-answer session at a public meeting. The protagonist raises her hand to ask a question that's important to her. Someone else is called on. She lowers her hand. She tries this a couple more times, but is still not called upon. She feels frustration, and her own tension builds. Finally, after being passed over yet again, she decides to just leave her hand in the air. The reader thinks that surely this will succeed. She's ignored again. Finally she waves her hand and gets to ask her question. So, while the main tension in the story was building at a slower rate, there was still pressure.

ADD CHARACTER SPIN TO CREATE TENSION

Every couple of years, a political season inundates us with politicians spinning each other's words and positions in order to distort and contrast them. I once hated the idea of spin . . . until it occurred to me that spin is a terrific way to create drama in a story. Spin comes from agendas, intentions, and beliefs of characters. When characters want something in every scene and words and actions are guided by conflicting agendas, you automatically generate tension, and characters boil with action and dialogue.

The way the doc in the following cartoon spins the facts reveals his bias and agenda.

Sol Stein, in *Stein on Writing*, uses the idea of agendas as "scripts" when he talks about the Actors Studio method for developing drama.

For example, let's say Faith, a compulsive gambler, is accused of murdering a sleazy bookmaker. Her lover, Percy, believes that Faith can do no wrong. Daggett, the district attorney, believes Faith is a liar who will do anything to get rid of a staggering debt to the bookmaker. On the surface, Percy and Daggett share a goal: to learn the truth. But differences in their internal views and agendas spin what they think, say, and do . . .

> Percy screeches his car to a halt in front of the brownstone. Faith had sounded frightened and desperate when she called. Rushing from his car, he finds her being led out the front door by the district attorney, Daggett.
>
> Faith's dress hangs in tatters and a bruise swells on her cheek. She staggers, and Percy races up the steps to steady her. Holding one arm as Daggett holds the other, Percy says, "My God. He tried to kill you!"
>
> Daggett shakes his head. "That's what she hopes we'll think." He wrenches Faith's arms behind her back and hobbles her wrists with handcuffs.

Poor Faith. Spin also applies to how characters interpret information. For example, in politics your orientation will add spin to the words "embryonic stem-cell research" that turns them into anathema, a blessing, or something in between. The same goes for your characters. And if two characters have different agendas, think what that can mean.

Percy believes Faith is innocent and wants to protect her, Daggett believes she's guilty down to the marrow of her bones and wants to convict her. They will interpret whatever she says and does differently depending on these beliefs. So here's how those two characters spin the exact same input.

> Faith's determined expression wavers, then breaks. "I'm guilty. I did it."
>
> Percy shakes his head. She must be covering for someone. "How can you say that, Faith?" He glances at Daggett, who wears a smile that reminds Percy of a bear trap.

> Daggett says, "Because she's guilty, guilty, guilty."

Clearly, agendas that are at cross-purposes spin up terrific tension. So ask each character in a scene these two questions:

- What's your agenda in this situation?
- What do you believe the other character's agenda is?

Then let 'em duke it out . . . and don't let either of them win, at least not for a few chapters.

UNSETTLE HAPPY SCENES WITH FUTURE JEOPARDY

Writer/agent Donald Maass writes of a need for tension on every page. Every page? Can't a character have a happy time now and then? Not really, at least not unmitigated happiness, not if you want to compel. If there isn't trouble in a scene, the reader must anticipate trouble to come.

By the way, some folks conflate "tension on every page" with "conflict on every page." Not the same.

The ironic humor in the cartoon comes from the reader knowing about danger ahead that the characters don't.

In a narrative, you can build tension by giving the reader knowledge about danger ahead that the protagonist doesn't have. It's a sure way to create continuous micro-tension on every page.

For example, here's an innocent-seeming scene:

Steve gunned the engine and the boat surged forward. Laura rose from the water on her skis, unsteady at first, but gaining control. She was able to give him a quick wave and a big smile.

Steve started a turn that would take her past the dam where the lake cascaded into the canyon below. Spray cooled her sun-warm skin and the speed thrilled. The force of the turn sent her arcing out behind the boat, swinging wide alongside the spillway and gaining speed.

She couldn't have been more alive, nor more in love.

Everything sounds loverly, but what if the writer has previously planted this:

Steve is a serial killer who romances women and then kills them, and water is always an element in his *modus operandi.*

Because of this foreknowledge, the reader will feel tension from the moment Laura gets into that boat, and it will only build. Is she headed over the lip of that dam? Heck, if she survives this and they go out to dinner, even Steve asking for glasses of water will be suspicious—what's he going to do with it? What's going to happen next?

You could call this a long slow-burning fuse of continuous micro-tension. You plant a bomb, light the fuse, and then carry on with the reader tensed for the explosion.

And then you put it off . . . and off . . . and off . . .

You don't have to create overt conflict on every page—a story with strong stakes and consequences makes it possible to use impending conflict or jeopardy to keep building tension in a reader.

There will be tension on every page even without direct conflict. Have those happy moments, but create "when-will-the-trouble-I-know-is-coming-strike" story questions that foreshadow trouble which will damage or diminish the protagonist.

SHIFT TO A DIFFERENT CHARACTER'S POV

Donald Maass suggests that ending a chapter at a moment of suspense and then shifting to another character's point of view for the next chapter is a good way to build tension.

It is. Try taking a scene to a moment of suspense in one character's point of view and then, at the point of maximum "what happens next?" go to a different character in a new scene. The following happens at the end of a *Hiding Magic* chapter (Annie uses a kind of magic to disguise herself as shadows):

> The woman aims her gun at them and calls out, "Department of Homeland Security. Hands up!"
>
> Gabe raises his hands. Annie becomes shadows. The agent fires her pistol into the air. The pistol lowers to aim at Annie. "I can see what you do. Stop your tricks!"
>
> Annie's shadows disappear and she backs against the railing. "Oh, what have I done?" She wraps her arms around her abdomen and bends as if bearing a crushing weight.
>
> Gabe steps close and puts his arm around her shoulders, careful to keep his other hand raised. He draws her to him.
>
> The agents advance, their weapons scary, the grim hostility on their faces even scarier.

The next chapter opens this way:

After a morning of fuming at Vixen for her intransigence and at the bacteria on a slide for the same damnable characteristic, Drago powers off the electron microscope. Maybe he can get her to work on it one more time—no, she isn't going to forgive him for smashing her phone.

So we are left with wondering what's going to happen to Annie and Gabe, who are clearly in trouble, and go to a relatively calm scene with another character. The difference in intensity helps to heighten the sense of urgency we felt in the Annie/Gabe scene. The new chapter builds its own tension while the other is poised in the background, our minds tapping a mental foot and keeping those pages turning.

Just for fun, one more example of future jeopardy at work to create a what-happens-next moment (and a laugh):

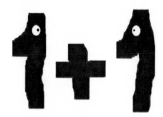

Creating the care factor

READERS DEMAND A PROTAGONIST that they can care about. I know this from personal experience in a critique group. After reading the opening pages of my novel that introduced a character, one criticism was "I don't care about her."

I knew that the character came across as cold and distant, and I explained that I'd written her that way on purpose so that there could be a character arc, so that the character could change and become more likeable.

My critiquer said,

> "Maybe I will care about her. But I don't. And I need that to want to keep reading about her."

Lesson learned. I changed the opening to include a small incident that created a little bit of a "care factor" for the character to soften her cold side. Think of this is as the "connect factor."

You don't have to expect the reader to like a character, but you need for them to connect. Literary agent Donald Maass says that where most good manuscripts fall short is in the middle—editors tell him that manuscripts "lost steam." One big reason: failure to engage the reader with the protagonist, and Maass advises that the connection should begin on the *first* page.

Thus it comes to pass that readers, literary agents, and acquisitions editors at publishing houses demand that your manuscript and mine have that characteristic. But how do you make it happen?

RELATIONSHIPS

Lou Aronica, an editor and the publisher of scores of best-selling novels, told me that the number one way to create caring for a character is to show the character in a relationship. This is not, he stressed, to make a reader like a character, but to create empathy, a person-to-person connection that can cause a reader to care about what happens to a character, even one that is otherwise not appealing. We all have relationships, and experiencing one on the page makes the character more "like us." I read a novel in which the protagonist was a pedophile and killer, and while the character was disgusting in many ways, there were sides of him with which I empathized.

Here's just such a character: Born-Again Bobby, who, when you meet him, is an obese, slovenly, crude, arrogant, corrupt religious leader. Yet by the end of the novel, you care about him. The caring begins with this—he goes to a facility where his little sister lives.

Bobby found Sadie at the shuffle-board court, crowing and clapping her chubby hands at knocking her opponent's puck off the ten-spot.

He called out, "Little sister."

She spun, and when she saw him a huge smile glowed. She ran to him, her clumsy gait typical of the short-legged, heavy body of Down Syndrome. Sadie threw herself at Bobby with arms open for a huge hug. He returned it with equal vigor. Comforted and rewarded by her unconditional love, his troubles left him.

Bobby left behind all thoughts of being the man liberals labeled "the leader of the nation's most volatile right-wing Christian sect." He was a big brother, happily spending the next five hours with his twenty-year-old little sister, pushing her in the swing, laughing on the teeter-totter, dancing, and playing go fish.

EVEN DEAD PEOPLE COUNT

Gundown opens with the protagonist deep in an emotional fugue—he doesn't really feel anything. And he's a gun for hire, able to kill with only a minor qualm.

So how can a reader feel empathy for a character that feels nothing? Through a scene that establishes a relationship and tugs at the reader just enough to understand the troubled nature of the man. From the chapter that introduces him:

> *The lovely woman laughed and swung the beautiful child back and forth.*
>
> *Words came from Jake, but he couldn't make them out because they were muddled and slow as if made of molasses.*
>
> *The woman frowned at him. She pulled the child close and said more molasses words that made no sense. The look on her face was angry. Wild.*
>
> *Insane.*
>
> *The beautiful child was in danger.*
>
> *He reached for his gun, so slowly . . .*
>
> A nasty mechanical buzz blasted him. Jake groped and turned off his alarm clock, and then fell back onto his pillow. He realized that he was holding his breath, his jaws clenched.

Why?

As he did every morning, he turned to a snapshot in a plain black frame on his nightstand—Amy in her favorite flowery party dress, forever five years old. He touched the tiny silver butterfly hanging on the frame by its chain. She had been wearing it the day she—

The butterfly glittered, and he couldn't bear to look at her any more.

He swung out of bed and his foot came down on an empty wine bottle. God, his head hurt—the price of self-medication. He scowled at all the damn sunshine coming in the window.

Outside, fat clouds in a sepia sky drifted over Lake Michigan. On the water, white triangles of sails leaned before the wind. Thirty stories below, sunlight flared from ant trails of cars on Lake Shore Drive. Most days he felt like an ant, mindlessly marching toward an unknown destination, especially since the numbness in his mind had set in right after Amy was—

His mental anesthetic choked off that line of thought.

In the bathroom, his red, puffy eyes bleared at him from the medicine-cabinet mirror. He wondered about the moisture on his cheeks. More and more, he found it there when he woke up. He touched it with a fingertip and then tasted. Salty.

The numbness said it didn't matter.

His grief for his dead daughter shows a deep and caring relationship.

ANOTHER CARE FACTOR: PASSION

Aronica told me that a second trait that can create a caring connection with a character is passion for achieving something. People driven to achieve or fighting for a cause bigger than themselves are things we can admire, and that brings the character closer to us. "Passion" is a facet of the "desire" I've talked about.

In the film *Rocky*, his passion for making the best of himself for the big fight takes him and the audience through rigorous training. The audience works with him every bit of the way, and then celebrates with him when he makes his triumphal run up the steps.

In Ayn Rand's *The Fountainhead*, Howard Roark's passion for his designs and for his vision of what they could be even in the face of crushing opposition creates a "rooting factor."

Passion is a character factor that can work with both protagonists and antagonists. In the film *Spider-Man 2*, Doctor Octopus has a goal of achieving a new energy source, which is admirable. Unfortunately, he goes a little nuts about it and does bad things to get there, but his fundamental passion is positive, and that keeps a human core alive inside him, and we can care about him when he sacrifices his life to save the city.

LASTLY, CARING ABOUT OTHERS

Showing a character caring is perhaps a form of having a relationship, but I think it's distinct enough to point out. Here's an example of putting that to work for an antagonist.

Wait, an antagonist? The bad guy? Caring? You bet. Sure, you can have a purely evil villain, and readers can enjoy the ride. But a novel has more depth and dimension when the antagonist is also seen as human by the reader. If a reader has just a little bit of connection with the opposition, then the lessons of how not to be a human being are more valid and valuable.

So, if you can create connections between your reader and

your antagonist, the story has set another hook, and the reader is drawn in more deeply.

Here's an illustration of caring. You've met Drago from *Hiding Magic*, and at that time you saw no clue that he will eventually do very bad things. It would be nice for the reader to be on his side, even if only a little bit, so his arc into evil will be greater and more meaningful. Here's how the chapter that introduces Drago opens (*lledri* is the energy used to create a *glamère*, the casting of an illusion):

> The percussive *whup-whup-whup* of a helicopter draws Drago to a porthole in his galleon's quarterdeck cabin. In the forest clearing where his ship and two others of his clan rest, a half-dozen clan children, teens to toddlers, build a snowman.
>
> The tall curved hulls of the sixteenth-century Spanish vessels, all grace when they sail through the air, now seem awkward, supports angling out like spider legs to hold them upright. The daylight is depressingly dim under the gray January sky, but that doesn't seem to matter to the children.
>
> The helicopter nears and the noise smothers their giggles. The galleons vanish behind *glamères* of snow-clad forest, the illusions broadcast by alert sentries.
>
> All save one of the children disappear as well, disguised as young trees. Little Alexandra, her *lledri* skills not yet awakened, bursts into tears. Drago swings the porthole open to help her with a concealing *glamère*, but then a sapling scoops up the child. In the flicker of a thought, a fat

squirrel appears in her place. Satisfied, he closes the port against the chill.

This man's instinctive move to protect a child says something about his values. Only later will the reader learn of his murderous desire for vengeance against ordinary humans. And it took very little narrative space to add this grace note to his character.

Remember the "cold" character that my critique partner didn't care for? She was Annie in *Hiding Magic*. Here's a trimmed-down version of the scene where the care factor was introduced (*sight* is the use of *lledri*, the organic magical ability in the story, and *lessi* is a word meaning people without the magical ability):

The Chicago Art Institute lobby welcomes me with an expanse of beige marble that prompts admiration for its grandeur, although I would rather see the meadow that once opened here, cloaked with snow in wintertime, its future a summer of green grass and golden flowers. There was a time when I walked a deer path through that meadow to the lake beyond that seems as vast as an ocean.

A voice behind me calls out, "Jimmy! Stop!" A boy of about seven zooms past and glances back, grinning. His foot hits a spot of melt from tracked-in snow, and I wince at the jagged red-orange burst of pain in his aura when his head slams the marble floor.

Two long steps and I kneel beside him. His eyes widen, tears spill, and a wail echoes from the marble walls. I stroke his head as I slip my *sight* under his scalp and locate a growing contusion. Drawing on the streams of *lledri* energy coursing around me, I stop the bleeding beneath his skin and clear out the damaged cells. Soon pain nerves quiet and the injury is on the way to healing.

The boy stops crying just as his mother arrives and drops to her knees beside him. She says, "Are you okay?"

The boy sniffles, glances up at me—I smile—and he nods. The mother says to me, "Thank you."

I nod and then make my way to the cashiers to pay my admission. Having seen the boy fall, I instinctively take care on the slippery floor—and then grimace at the irony. What matters a bruise to a corpse?

Create a really good bad guy

I'M BRINGING VLADIMIR back to illustrate creating a "good" antagonist. By that I mean a strong, interesting, and maybe even likeable character. Here's what we know of good old Vlad so far:

> Vladimir's blade sliced open Johnson's throat. The child-killer toppled, hands clutching his neck. Vladimir watched him writhe, and then become still. The bittersweet taste of vengeance filled Vladimir, and he smiled.

He has killed, but for a good reason—maybe. At this point, Vladimir could be the protagonist or the antagonist, although a reader is likely to be rooting for anyone who kills a child-killer. In this initial ambiguity lies a key to creating a good bad guy. We'll return to Vladimir later to resolve the ambiguity with more of the narrative.

It's easy to create a bad bad guy—you make him evil through and through, corrupt, cruel, cowardly. You use action and word choice to paint an unredeemable baddie.

I did just that with my first novel at the beginning of my learning curve. Luckily, when I decided to publish it, I did something that all indie authors should do: hire an editor. Yes, I'm an editor, but that has taught me how blind all authors can be to narrative flaws.

That was when I hired editor and publisher Lou Aronica. His critique exposed a problem with the primary antagonist. Lou said he wasn't strong enough or smart enough to be an interesting character, and I finally understood that he was right.

I didn't like the bad guy and I didn't want my readers to like him either. So I had made all of his characteristics unlikable—he was weak, corrupt, greedy, cowardly, dishonest, arrogant, and not all that bright.

So how do you write a guy you really don't like as appealing?

An "aha" experience arrives

Finally it hit me. I needed to treat the antagonist like a protagonist. After all, he is the protagonist in his story, right? He believes in what he does, and that he's doing the right thing. It doesn't matter that I disagree with him or that the things he will do are evil. What matters is that for him they are the right thing to do, and that his cause is just.

We're all like that, aren't we? Even when we do something we know is wrong, we do it anyway because, at that moment in our lives, it's the right thing to do. Think of that second helping of chocolate cake you knew you shouldn't eat . . .

Bad guys don't think of themselves as bad guys. They're the heroes. So a narrative in deep third person POV that intimates that this person is bad and what he's doing is nefarious isn't true to character. And it's character that makes a story compelling.

Take Vladimir. He seems to have excellent motivation for brutally killing a man. He clearly believes that it's the right thing to do. Since the victim had killed a child, we may even be on his side, emotionally.

But what if it develops that his victim is a doctor who has

performed legal abortions that Vladimir opposes? Or perhaps, less controversial, a surgeon whose child patient died in surgery though no fault of his own? And this is the fifth surgeon Vladimir has killed? So now good old Vlad is a serial killer, and a very sick puppy.

I'm sure I had read advice on thinking about an antagonist as the star of his own story, but I had never internalized it. Once this epiphany finally hit—and I imagine that for many of you this is old hat—I started thinking again about how to portray my good/bad guy. The way the narrative delivers what he thinks and does shouldn't signal that he or his actions are evil, because, to him, they're not. And if the reader starts out feeling some empathy for this guy and his goals, then the arc of his story will be bigger and more dramatic.

Also, the smarter and stronger the bad guy is, the stronger the conflict, and the stronger the protagonist will be when he finally wins. Greater conflict! Bigger stakes! More tension!

The point is, once I viewed the world from inside his (now smarter) head, even my word choices changed. The way he reacts to people and events in his world changed. From his viewpoint, I was able to see the story's good guy as a bad guy.

Holy schizophrenia!

I must confess that it's difficult to shift the narrative and exposition—the word choices—from painting a picture of a nasty guy to one of someone who isn't, as far as we can tell. But that kind of ambiguity helps create a character with depth. By the way, it's also a good tactic to create unlikable aspects in your good guys to create richer characters.

Here is how the hero version of my antagonist is introduced.

> In his hotel room, Kurt knotted his tie and then cocked his thumb and aimed an index-finger gun barrel at Noah Stone's smile.

Stone looked up at the fingertip muzzle from the cover of a *Time* magazine on the dresser; the headline read, "The Alliance's Pied Piper."

Kurt squeezed the trigger and wished for a hole in the enemy's forehead.

Like Daddy used to say, if wishes were horses, beggars would ride. He shook his head.

His cell phone rang. The president's gravelly voice said, "New poll in, Kurt, and that Alliance son of a bitch's killing us out West. Have you got the attorney general moving on Noah Stone yet?"

"Meeting with her and our man in just a few minutes, Mr. President."

The president said, "This is a matter of national interest, Kurt."

Damn right it was. Their opponents were blatantly abrogating Second Amendment rights. As far as Kurt was concerned, weakening America in this troubled world amounted to treason.

Kurt flicked a glance at the *Time* cover. "I'll do whatever it takes, sir." Noah Stone was an evil SOB. His ideas were toxic, and his initiatives stole basic American rights.

If ever there was a man who was an enemy of freedom, that man was Noah Stone. Kurt had a duty to stop him.

Kurt's passion for the kind of country he thinks is right, his love for the president, and, of course, weaknesses, cause this character to orchestrate events that lead to the assassination of a good man—the Noah Stone referred to is one of the good guys. But at this point, you don't know that, do you?

Kurt is a good bad guy.

It's the words.

I think Stephen King is a master at generating mood and tension by using a micro approach to word choice to create the right effect. This first struck me years ago in his novel, *'Salem's Lot*. His chapter one opens this way:

> By the time he had passed Portland going north on the turnpike, Ben Mears had begun to feel a not unpleasurable tingle of excitement in his belly. It was September 5, 1975, and summer was enjoying her final grand fling. The trees were bursting with green, the sky was a high, soft blue, and just over the Falmouth town line he saw two boys walking a road parallel to the expressway with fishing rods settled on their shoulders like carbines.

It's a cheerful scene with greenery, blue skies, and boys, and with words such as enjoying and grand. But just a few pages later the mood changes.

> A big BSA cycle with jacked handlebars suddenly roared past him in the passing lane, a kid in a T-shirt driving, a girl in a red cloth jacket and huge mirror-lensed sunglasses riding pillion behind him. They cut in a little too quickly and he overreacted, jamming on his brakes and laying both hands on the horn. The BSA sped up, belching blue smoke from its exhaust, and the girl jabbed her middle finger back at him.

Not only the action but the word choices shift the mood: belching, jabbing. And then later:

A sudden blackness came over him, dousing his good spirits like sand on fire. He had been subject to these since (his mind tried to speak Miranda's name and he would not let it) the bad time and was used to fending them off, but this one swept over him with a savage power that was dismaying.

Again, note the word choices: blackness, dousing, savage, dismaying. King is a master of writing for effect.

Haunt characters for stronger storytelling

WHEN I WAS IN HOLLYWOOD working on breaking into screenwriting, I took courses. One was Robert McKee's excellent workshop. Another was from a different screenwriting master, John Truby. McKee's was all about structure. But Truby got into other aspects of storytelling, including characterization.

An idea from his course that has stuck with me and proved useful is his notion that characters should have a "ghost." We're not talking about a haunt from Casper the Friendly Ghost, but a powerful, transformative event in a character's past that, whether consciously or not, affects his current behavior.

A now-clichéd example is childhood abuse suffered by a serial killer. It's a true-to-life ghost, but nowadays is becoming ho-hum. Authors may work to make their character's abuse more unique and horrific than competing killers, but it remains a standard serial-killer ingredient. And it is used to motivate the behavior of other troubled characters, and rightfully so—abuse is a powerful "ghost."

A violent ghost such as abuse is a good motivator for an antagonist, but I look for other things to trouble my characters. I'm most concerned with finding ghosts for my protagonists. I seek to write about flawed characters, and for me a ghost is one of the best ways to create a weak spot in a character.

My character ghosts are usually deep-seated and not necessarily conscious. The primary requirement is that it—the past event—still influences behavior. I don't necessarily make my readers aware of the ghost, certainly not early on. But, to have credible motivation, aspects of the haunt need to be revealed along the way. If conquering the ghost is part of the character's final epiphany, then it will be revealed.

Here's a tragic ghost for one of my primary protagonists. Jake shot and killed his wife in an unsuccessful attempt to save the life of his five-year-old daughter who his wife, in the grip of psychosis, has killed. He deeply loved his wife, and the event was so traumatic that he has no conscious memory of it. He knows the facts—they were all in the police report—but he cannot recall what happened. It is, however, the content of a recurring nightmare—you saw the scene a few pages back in the chapter on creating the care factor.

More than that, this ghost has caused a kind of fugue in Jake—his emotions have shut down entirely to prevent further emotional injury. If you don't love someone, they can't hurt you.

This ghost in Jake's past affects everything in his day-to-day life: his relationships with other people, especially women; how he reacts to small children; and how he lives his professional life. He is an ex Secret Service agent turned mercenary, able to kill without conscious remorse or hesitation. Note that I said "conscious;" his ghost affects even his reaction to killing and leaves him feeling nauseated after he kills.

Jake has an unconscious desire to break the thrall of his fugue and to conquer his ghost. When cracks begin to appear as a result of what happens to him in the course of the novel, he is eventually drawn to widening them and, finally, taking a gigantically risky route to conquering his ghost. When it is at last exorcised, his behavior changes, and that affects the climax of the story.

In my novel, *The Summer Boy,* a coming-of-age mystery, the seventeen-year-old hero is haunted by the death of his father. It is more conscious in this story, but still an event that affects his thinking and motivates behavior, especially during the climactic conflict. Here's the key scene; note that it uses a mini-flashback.

Jesse wanted to smash his fists into . . . into . . . himself. Because he was running away. Somebody had killed his best friend in the world, and he was running home to Mama. He closed his eyes, and his father's face rose in his mind.

His dad had noticed the bruises on Jesse's arm when he picked Jesse up from Jefferson Elementary School. "How did you get those?"

Jesse had cast his gaze down. "I dunno."

"Jesse?"

He had to tell. "It's Ryan. He's big, and the teachers never catch him."

His father had thought, and then he'd shook his head. "I'll talk to the principal about it."

"Please don't, Daddy. I'll stay away from him."

"It's not right, son, it's not right."

The next morning, his dad had gone to school and told the principal all about it.

The following day, Ryan's father had stomped up the steps to their front porch and hammered on their door. He yelled, "Your kid's a goddam liar!"

Jesse's dad had said, quietly, "Bruises don't lie." Later, Jesse had thought maybe it was his father's calm that made Ryan's father grab Jesse's dad by his tie and yank him off the porch.

Jesse's father hit the sidewalk wrong and broke his neck. He had died right in front of Jesse, surprise in his dead eyes. He died because he hadn't been able to rest knowing a wrong needed righting.

His father wouldn't be smiling now. Jesse couldn't let his dad down. Before the night was over, he would tell Sheriff Webb what was wrong at the ranch and then do whatever the sheriff said.

I urge you to find a ghost for your most important "un-haunted" characters, even if you're already into your project. You may be surprised at how it can change your character's reactions to the events and barriers you throw into her path along the way.

WHAT ARE THOSE LITTLE WEIRD THINGS IN TAPIOCA PUDDING

It takes story questions to turn pages

I HAVE BECOME CONVINCED, especially after critiquing more than 800 first chapters on my blog, that story questions are the essential ingredient for crafting a compelling narrative—you can also think of them as "plot questions." To keep a reader reading—especially an agent or editor overwhelmed with submissions—a narrative must continually spark story questions in a reader's mind. Emphasis on continually: please, no scenic side trips.

There's no more important time to sprout questions than when your novel opens. I learn best by example, so I thought a look at how some of the pros do it might be helpful to you. These are from books on my shelves.

Anne Rice opens *The Witching Hour* with this:

> The doctor woke up afraid. He had been dreaming of the old house in New Orleans again. He had seen the woman in the rocker. He'd seen the man with the brown eyes.
>
> And even now in this quiet hotel room above New York City he felt the old alarming disorientation. He'd been talking again with the brown-haired man. Yes, help her. No, this is just a dream. I want to get out of it.

Even the first sentence raises a story question: Why is the doctor afraid?

I was enthralled by Alice Sebold's *The Lovely Bones*. Here's how it drew me in with a story question provoked by the second sentence.

> My name was Salmon, like the fish; first name, Susie. I was fourteen when I was murdered on December 6, 1973. In newspaper photos of missing girls from the seventies, most looked like me: white girls with mousy brown hair. This was before kids of all races and genders started appearing on milk cartons or in the daily mail. It was still back when people believed things like that didn't happen.

If that voice alone isn't enough to hook you, don't you just have to keep reading long enough to find out what happened to Susie? And note that the author slips in an "active" description of the point-of-view character in the context of the story question and the character's thoughts.

I like openings that involve you with the protagonist right away. Here's the opening from *The Footprints of God,* by Greg Iles. The first paragraph raises a question that forces you to read further.

> "My name is David Tennant, M.D. I'm professor of ethics at the University of Virginia Medical School, and if you're watching this tape, I'm dead."

Story questions don't, however, have to be limited to what's happening plot-wise; they can be about the character. Here's how

Pulitzer Prize winner Carol Shields opens *Unless*:

> It happens that I am going through a period of great unhappiness and loss just now. All my life I've heard people speak of finding themselves in acute pain, bankrupt in spirit and body, but I've never understood what they meant. To lose. To have lost. I believed these visitations of darkness lasted only a few minutes or hours and that these saddened people, in between bouts, were occupied, as we all were, with the useful monotony of happiness. But happiness is not what I thought. Happiness is the lucky pane of glass you carry in your head. It takes all your cunning just to hang on to it, and once it's smashed you have to move into a different sort of life.

We've all suffered loss and unhappiness, and the story questions for me include wondering what caused hers and how she would deal with it.

Harlen Coben begins *No Second Chance* with this:

> When the first bullet hit my chest, I thought of my daughter.
>
> At least, that is what I want to believe. I lost consciousness pretty fast. And, if you want to get technical about it, I don't even remember being shot. I know that I lost a lot of blood. I know that a second bullet skimmed the top of my head, though I was probably already out by then. I know that my heart stopped. But I still like to think that as I lay dying, I thought of Tara.

The opening of one of my novels, *The Vampire Kitty-cat Chronicles.*

> Just after dark, death grabbed me by the tail.
> The moon was full, and the earthy scent of fall
> flavored a cool September breeze. My mind on a
> svelte little Siamese who was coming into heat,
> I trotted over a mound of fresh dirt, not an un-
> common thing in a graveyard, and a hand shot
> up and grabbed my rear extremity.

Are you ready to put the book down? (I hope not. How embarrassing.)

So how does the opening of your novel compare to the examples above? It doesn't have to be similar in technique—these vary widely—but it does have to raise questions that are going to make your mind itch for a good scratch that only the story can give.

Once you've got your novel launched, the narrative has to do two things:

1. Answer some of the questions you raise
2. Bring up new ones—like a bird following a trail of seeds, the reader sees the next seed just as he eats one . . . and so the story moves and pages turn

During the course of the story's middle, smaller questions are continually raised and answered to keep the tension in your reader alive and well. But you don't want your reader to reach the end of a chapter feeling that this would be a good place to put your book down. There should never be a good place to put your book down.

Chapter endings

A WRITER ONCE ASKED ME THIS:

> "How about chapter endings? Must they always end with a cliff-hanging, hyperventilating, page-turning, stomach-churning, my-God-I-ripped-the-pages-trying-to-find-what-comes-next? I just realized my ms is structured chronologically and some chapters seem to end naturally with everyone going to sleep at the end of a day, and I'm looking for excuses to leave it as it is."

I know what she was facing. The story is moving along. A chapter seems solid, it advances the plot, or characterizes, or both. It feels good. But the ending isn't something that clenches your mental knuckles. Is that a problem? Not if you have underlying tension from before that's building.

Agent Cherry Weiner once took a look at an early novel of mine, a Western mystery. Her rejection letter told me that "the characters were good and the story was interesting. But I could put it down." I have yet to rewrite that novel, but I will.

That's what readers and agents and acquisitions editors are looking for—something they don't want to put down. How hard is that to do, if the story is interesting and the characters good? Apparently my Western didn't have the answer.

I know I haven't answered the original question yet, but context is important. An agent has requested a manuscript based on a query letter, so it's sorta screened (a great query letter does not always lead directly to a great read). She's received hundreds of submissions, many of which are interesting or have good characters. The brain cells the woman uses to evaluate fiction have calluses. What do you think it's going to take to create a story she doesn't want to stop reading?

And she knows something you don't—the fiction market is so tight and so tough that many acquisitions editors are turning more and more to nonfiction just to find something they feel they can recommend for publication. Your novel has to be something that keeps these equally jaded readers from setting the manuscript aside.

Keep in mind that this book is about compelling storytelling. I think that to succeed with fiction in today's market, every chapter must compel the reader to turn the page because they gotta know what happens next.

Does this necessarily mean that every chapter must "always end with a cliff-hanging, hyperventilating, page-turning, stomach-churning, my-God-I-ripped-the-pages-trying-to-find-what-comes-next?"

What every story must do, whether at chapter beginning, middle, or end, is raise story questions that are so provocative, so engaging, so rife with intrigue that the reader is compelled to keep reading. When I reread the novel that Cherry Weiner rejected, I came to places where I felt I could put it down. She was right. I sent it to my then agent and, even though he loved the two novels of mine he was representing at the time, he couldn't seem to finish reading that one. I haven't spent the time to figure out how to fix it yet, but that's the tough truth.

Story questions can be cumulative; they can add up to create an overriding level of tension in the reader. It's that level of tension that carries readers through exposition and description. And I think it can affect the reader's take on how a fairly benign chapter ends.

Midway into *Hiding Magic*, a protagonist has just escaped torture and death at the hands of a not-so-ethical Homeland Security agent. The reader knows that he will continue to be pursued. He can't return to his life. He's lost his job. He's on the run. And the reader knows much more about the character that makes her want him to be okay.

The reader also knows that the man who helped our hero escape has a nefarious use for him that will lead to the deaths of many people. In this context, the protagonist reaches what seems to be a safe haven with his rescuer. He is cared for and, even more fun, is seduced by a beautiful, provocative woman. The chapter ends in the midst of their love-making. For this character, a very happy ending.

So the chapter doesn't literally end with a cliff-hanger, but the story questions already in the reader's mind are so powerful by then that putting those questions on hold for a moment of peace actually increases the tension in the reader because she knows trouble is coming, bigtime. Another example of continuous micro-tension.

And therein lies the best answer I have for the question. It may be fine for a chapter to end without people dangling over the edge of a precipice if the reader knows that terrible trouble is inevitable and coming on strong.

The non-cliffhanger chapter must still be riveting in its own way, with unanticipated twists and turns that keep story questions coming. And I don't think you can defer getting back to the white-knuckle part for too long, else the reader will put your book down.

In some texts on screenwriting it's suggested that if act one ends on a negative note for the protagonist, then act two should end positively. It is the contrast that helps create tension. Stories must have rising tension, but along the way there should be brief respites. Without valleys, there are no peaks.

However, all that said, I'm going to work darned hard to make sure that every chapter I write (and edit) does end with a clear sense of compelling tension.

I think you owe it to all the work you've done on your novel to step back, take a look, and use your talent as a storyteller to make sure the tension crackles throughout the narrative. I'll bet you can end those going-to-sleep chapters with tension quivering. If it's difficult for you to see where the narrative needs injections of pressure, find informed, story-smart fresh eyes to help you see. We all need fresh eyes to make judgments about tension and story questions because we just can't totally trust our own. We know too much and we love our stories too much to see the saggy places.

AUTHOR   EDITOR

You have to go beyond strong writing

CHUCK ADAMS, EXECUTIVE EDITOR of Algonquin Books, says,

> "There's a lot of good writing, but that doesn't
> necessarily add up to a good book."

Story is the thing, but not just any old story told in an ordinary way. You need something that somehow takes you to a place you never thought about going.

Here's what Kristin Nelson, literary agent, said in her blog.

> I've been reading a lot of fulls lately and
> it occurred to me that there are a lot of strong
> writers out there—writers with enough talent
> to break into publishing, but the current manu-
> scripts I'm reviewing probably won't be the ones
> to open the door.
>
> I think writers assume that good writing is
> enough. Well, it's not. You have to couple good
> writing with an original storyline—something
> that will stand out as fresh and original. A story
> never told in this way before (even if elements
> are similar to what is already out on the market).

Case in point: when I was in Hollywood working on screen-writing, I got good at writing screenplays. Agents and others gave me feedback that let me know I had mastered the form.

I acquired an agent, and my scripts had all the elements: good dialogue; good action; good tension; good descriptions.

I was frustrated when nothing sold, but much later I came to realize what my scripts lacked: stories strong enough to make someone invest a couple of years and millions of dollars into making a movie about them.

I was story-impaired. This is not to say that they weren't good, interesting stories. They were. But they didn't take you to places you'd never dreamed of in particularly dramatic or special ways.

The television series we watch can get away with stories that reek of familiarity because they're free to us. You don't have to invest much in a TV series story. But a book—you pay hard cash and then spend all that time reading.

The agent you're hoping to hook up with wants a story that will not let her put the book down. The manuscript an agent rejected because she could put it down suffered from a story problem, not a writing problem.

Harsh reality. When you submit a partial or full manu-script to an agent, you're asking her to invest her most valuable resource—her time. Think of a story as having cash value. You need to buy her time, and you'd better be ready to ante up some serious story value to pay for it.

The same goes with acquiring editors at publishing houses. Your submission is asking them to spend:

- Time—of which they don't have enough.
- Credibility—they have to sell your book to a committee, and then to the sales guys.
- Money—they've got to ask the company to spend thou-sands on getting your book to market.

All these people know that their target audiences want one thing—story.

Be tough on yourself and ask the hard question: Is my story unique enough . . . strong enough . . . fresh enough . . .

I look at my novels and, to be honest, I don't think a couple of them will ever rise far enough above the sea of submissions to snare a contract because of the size and natures of the stories.

But then there's *The Vampire Kitty-cat Chronicles,* which revolves around my unique take on the vampire legend. Since it concerns vampires, let's tune in to Kristin again.

> Recently, I had the pleasure of reading three full paranormal novels featuring Vampires. All three were really well written. Had interesting characters that were developed. And even had interesting twists to the Vampire plot to make it unique.
>
> Sounds good, right? So what happened?
>
> The scenes the writers chose to create (in order to unveil the plot) were almost identical in each novel. I literally could have taken scenes out of one novel and plopped them into another and it wouldn't have impacted the story much.

I wasn't worried about my vampire story until she listed some of the repetitive elements in the three novels. Her list starts with:

> 1. The backstory of how the vampire was made in the first place.

Dang. My novel starts with my hero being turned into a vampire. On the other hand, at least it's not backstory, it's the inciting incident.

And, heh-heh, the fresh thing is that the hero/narrator is a kitty-cat. Will that meet Kristin's criteria of "A story never told in this way before (even if elements are similar to what is already out on the market)"?

Another from her list:

> 2. Opening scene where the two main protago-
> nists (usually male and female) are enemies but
> somehow must break through the barrier to
> work together. This usually involves a violent,
> confrontational scene to jump-start the narra-
> tive. This scene usually happens in a dark place.

I do okay with number two—it's nighttime, but they're vampires. The initial scene where the other main protagonist turns my kitty-cat into a vampire is violent, but the next scene where he confronts her takes place in a convenience store, and there's no violence.

> 3. The main protagonists are being chased or
> must travel in order to accomplish what must
> be done. This is usually done in a car and there
> are motel/hotel scenes.

I'm good here, too. There's no chasing or traveling. In fact, my characters confront the whole societal enmity for vampires by coming out of the, er, grave.

Sounds pretty mundane when she abstracts scenes like that, doesn't it? My story doesn't exactly follow that pattern—except the darkness (hey, they're vampires)—so I feel I can hope that this will escape the curse of "oh, that again."

This reminds me of a lesson from somewhere along the line that had to do with screenwriting, but it applies equally well to a novel. Let's say you want to write a scene in which two people tell each other they love one another.

Imagine that scene set in a lovely restaurant, with great service by the waiter, music in the background, etc.

Pardon the yawn.

Now imagine the same scene at the side of a freeway, at night, in the rain, while the pair scrambles to change a flat tire as cars race past. Then there's a drive-by shot from a road-rager who pulls over and gets out of his truck. Don't you think the emotions, the dialogue, the action will be much more riveting?

Section 4: Workouts

AGENTS AND EDITORS REPORT that they look for reasons to reject, and that they can usually make that decision based on the first page, or perhaps two. With good justification, too—first pages foreshadow what follows, and after reading hundreds of submissions, these pros are attuned to distinct clues as to:

- The quality of writing that they will encounter
- The appeal of the voice
- Tension in the story

In a properly formatted novel manuscript—double-spaced, one-inch margins, 12-point type (I recommend Times New Roman)—chapters begin about a third of the way down the page. That translates into sixteen or seventeen lines of narrative.

Those lines can be make-or-break with an agent or acquisitions editor—or a book browser in a bookstore. You need to make it virtually impossible for them to resist reading on.

You must *compel* them to turn the page.

On my blog, *Flogging the Quill,* I do a critique called the "Flogometer." Writers send me their first chapter or prologue, and I challenge them to compel me and my readers to turn the page. Then I critique the sample for its strengths and shortcomings, doing some edits and making suggestions.

I put up a poll for readers to vote, and it's usually the most informative thing a writer will see—objective views of the strength of their opening page.

I ask for Yes, No, and Almost votes. While in the real world of book browsers and agents and editors the choices are actually Yes or No, for learning purposes I think an Almost vote is valuable in that it lets the writer know that they're close.

"Interests me" isn't a good enough reason for me to turn the page, and it can't be good enough for you. Your first sixteen or seventeen lines have to have the power to force a page turn. If they don't, your book risks being tossed.

Following are opening pages from chapters sent to me by people working hard at becoming published. I'll give you the opening double-spaced so there's room for you to make notes, add words, do edits that you feel are needed, and add comments or direction you would give about what works and what doesn't.

After you exercise your critical faculties, I'll give you the critique I did. Once you've finished this book, pull out the first sixteen lines of your novel and think about how well they meet the challenge.

Do the work

If you're like me, you may be tempted to just read the samples and then go on to the critiques. Trust me, that's not a good idea. I guarantee nothing will focus you on the merits and shortcomings of writing (including your own) like having a pencil in hand and the duty to edit.

I strongly urge you to strike through things you'd cut, add things you'd add, indicate where you might move pieces of narrative, and write in comments that help the writer. And don't forget to note things the writer does that you like.

You'll find yourself applying the lessons from this book and seeing a narrative in new ways—and that can lead to you seeing your own writing with far fresher eyes.

Answer the tough questions. Is it compelling? Does it hook you? Does the writing create an experience in your mind?

One of the things you'll learn from your work is the subjectivity of editing. You may find yourself with views that oppose mine.

But I think you'll also find plenty of agreement. Best of all, you'll begin to apply a critical and analytical eye to narrative, which can lead to clearer vision when you look at your own work.

KEEP IN MIND THE FIRST-PAGE CHECKLIST:

- It begins *connecting the reader with the protagonist.*
- *Something is happening.* This does NOT include a character musing about whatever.
- *What happens is dramatized* in an immediate scene with action and description plus, if it works, dialogue.
- What happens *moves the story forward.*
- What happens *has consequences* for the protagonist.
- The protagonist *desires something.*
- The protagonist *does something.*
- *There's enough of a setting* to orient the reader as to where things are happening.
- It *happens in the NOW* of the story.

- *Backstory? What backstory?* We're in the NOW of the story.
- *Set-up? What set-up?* We're in the NOW of the story.
- What happens *raises a story question*—what happens next? or why did that happen?

You'll find No, Almost, and Yes votes in the Workout samples. And you'll see how an Almost can rise to a Yes, and how a Yes can be made stronger. It's your task to see the ways to do the editing that can make those things happen.

Conventions I'll use to show editing:

- Deletions are shown with ~~strikethrough~~.
- Additions are **bold**.
- Comments are in parentheses and *(italicized)*.
- Phrases to think about are <u>underlined</u>.

Workout 1

THIS IS THE ONE FROM AUSTRALIA YOU SAW in the Benchmark chapter at the beginning of this book. Think back to your evaluation then. See if you see it differently this time around.

'Michael's gone!' Julia screamed into the payphone outside Flinders Street Train Station.

'Calm down, Mrs Stewart. She'll be with you shortly.'

Julia bristled at the matter-of-factness of the receptionist's voice. 'I don't care if she's with the Queen. My husband is missing. I think I'm losing my mind.'

'Please hold and I'll see if I can interrupt.'

Click. Mozart replaced the receptionist's voice. The familiar hold music from the past sounded surreal against the background tram and traffic noise of the Melbourne thoroughfare.

A pedestrian bumped into her daughter's stroller, turning Shellie to tears.

'Stop that, you bad girl!' Julia rolled the stroller under the phone box, putting her child out of the way of the Friday afternoon commuters.

Shellie reached out and cried louder.

'Arrgghh!' Julia dropped the receiver, picked up the three year old and settled her on her hip. Shellie quieted, distracted now by an earring.

Ignoring her, Julia reached for the dangling receiver, and found silence. 'Hello? Hello!' *Don't be gone. I don't have any more change.*

'I thought I'd lost you.' The receptionist's cheerfulness was enough to piss off anyone.

Would you turn the page? Mark up the sample with cuts, ideas, whatever you'd advise this writer to do to improve this narrative.

I VOTED YES. **I** WANTED TO SEE WHAT WAS NEXT

Good story questions, good writing, a likeable voice—all contributed to my turning the page. I like starting with a scene, and the very first line introduces an element of tension. However, I have thoughts for improvement. My notes:

Julia screamed 'Michael's gone!' ~~Julia screamed~~ into the payphone ~~outside Flinders Street Train Station~~. *(If you want the reader to get that 'Michael's gone!' is screamed, then you need to clue the reader first. I felt that naming the train station felt like an authorial intrusion here—she wouldn't be thinking of that. I'd leave it at the pay phone and mention the train station later.)*
'Calm down, Mrs Stewart. She'll be with you shortly.'
Julia bristled at the matter-of-factness of the receptionist's voice. 'I don't care if she's with the Queen. My husband is missing. I think I'm losing my mind.' *(While this seems okay, I wonder if it's enough. As it turns out, her husband has been missing for two hours, and she's pretty much panicked. "Bristle" seems too mild to be consistent with panic. A thought-starter: what about an internal rhetorical question, something like:* How could the damned receptionist be so matter-of-fact? Michael's missing! *'I don't care if she's . . .)*
'Please hold and I'll see if I can interrupt.'
~~Click.~~ Mozart replaced the receptionist's voice. The ~~familiar hold~~ music ~~from the past~~ sounded surreal against the background tram **and traffic noise** of the Melbourne thoroughfare **beside the Flinders Street Train Station**. *(The reference to "from the past" confused me, and it seemed to place more significance on the music than I think is necessary. As you see, here's where I'd work in the train station.)*
A pedestrian bumped into her daughter's stroller, turn-

ing Shellie to tears.

'Stop that, you bad girl!' Julia rolled the stroller under the phone box, putting her child out of the way of the Friday afternoon commuters.

Shellie ~~reached out and~~ cried louder.

'Arrgghh!' Julia dropped the receiver, picked up the three-year-old and settled her on her hip. Shellie quieted, distracted now by an earring. *(The "distracted" part is telling where this could be shown. For example:* Shellie toyed with an earring and quieted.*)*

~~Ignoring her,~~ Julia reached for the dangling receiver and found silence. 'Hello? Hello!' *Don't be gone. I don't have any more change.*

'I thought I'd lost you.' The <u>receptionist's cheerfulness</u> was enough to piss off anyone. *(While I agree that the tone might piss anyone off, I don't think that a woman in a state of panic would be thinking of that in this way. Thoughtstarter: what about something like this as a way to show her emotions and frame of mind?* Julia wanted to scream at the cheery voice, but choked it back.*)*

Nice work from Jan. I advised her to keep at it, focus on finding ways to show us, and to keep the protagonist's emotional state firmly in mind when she describes reactions, etc.

Workout 2

THE FIRST SIXTEEN LINES of Irene's YA paranormal novel:

A Gnome Takes A Club To My Knuckles

Until I lived at Helping Hand, my life was pretty normal.

There was school, baseball games, friends, and the usual

stuff. The plantation changed it all.

Angel, one of my friends there, said that the plantation

was on the between. Things crossed over like in the Bermuda

Triangle. Sometimes—as with the disappearance of Buddy

Knoll—the between just sucked someone or something into

itself as if it was hungry.

Mick Grady

My name's Michael Grady, but my friends call me Mick.

I'm fourteen. Aunt Liza brought me to The Helping Hand

Plantation on a Thursday afternoon in early June. Helping Hand is a temporary place for children who have a family, but their family can't take care of them for a while. Aunt Liza had lost her job, so I had to live there until she got back on her feet.

I was assigned to the North Swamp Dorm and my dorm mother, Ms. Porter, led me up a winding staircase and down a long hallway.

"All the children, except for Tate Thunder, are on a field trip to New Orleans today," she said, her shoes tapping a beat on the hardwood floor. "Tate hurt his leg playing basketball, so he's around somewhere." She stopped outside a door. "You're in here."

I stepped in and Ms. Porter disappeared down the hall. There were six twin beds, separated by a nightstand—three were on the right wall, three on the left. I spotted my luggage (snip)

Mark up the narrative and decide if you'd have turned the page. Hint: there's plenty of narrative destined to experience the delete key.

No go for me.

I'm sure some will disagree (remember how subjective this reading game is), but I wasn't compelled to turn the page. What, you might ask, stopped me, considering that enticing tidbit at the top about a kid's disappearance and the "between?" And what about the gnome?

Because that was the only really interesting stuff on the page. After the narrator told me (didn't show me) some information, we got into an entirely mundane arrival of a boy at a temporary housing site. Yes, he has difficulties, what with his Aunt Liza and all, but there doesn't seem to be much jeopardy attached. We see no trouble ahead.

I guess that, for me, this lacked the promise of a well-told story. First was the authorial intrusion to tell me things about this place that, I think, would have better been discovered. Second was the lack of tension in what followed.

It's not that this writer can't do that. In fact, she did just a sentence or two beyond her opening page. Cutting and rearranging just a little, here's what she had. Imagine the manuscript starting with these paragraphs:

> There were six twin beds, separated by night-stands—three on the right wall, three on the left. I spotted my luggage on the right middle bed. Fear crawled inside me and—just for a minute—I pictured myself stuck in this place for four years until I turned eighteen.
>
> "No," I said. Hot tears teased the corners of my eyes.
>
> I sat on the bed next to my luggage. That's when a tiny man jumped on the bed and beat on my hand with a small, wooden club.

Now, that was just six lines of narrative in manuscript form, and I'm a whole lot more hooked than I was by the original sixteen. All that stuff about where he is and why he's there can be handled by slipping it in with bits and pieces as this interesting scene develops.

Look at all the story questions raised in these six lines:

- Where is the boy?
- Why is he there?
- How could he be stuck there?
- Why does it make him cry?
- And what's with the tiny man whacking him on the hand?

This revised narrative even lets you know that the narrator is a boy of fourteen without "telling" us so. The only area needing improvement is the reference to "tiny" and "small wooden club." Tiny could be better defined — just how tiny is he? And what's "small" in the context of a "tiny" man? For example, what about showing us with specifics that make us visualize rather than telling us with something like:

> That's when a tiny man no taller than a teapot jumped on the bed and beat on my hand with a wooden club the size of a lollipop.

My advice to Irene was to skip all the explanations and get to the STORY. Find a way, with dialogue and internal monologue, to weave the rest in.

Workout 3

PATRICIA BATES SENT her opening to *Flogging the Quill* for a critique, and a few months later she wrote this to me:

> "I just wanted to drop you a line and say thank you for the flog you did for me some time ago. I took your advice and reworked the lines and the style a bit and now I am sitting on a contract with Champagne Books to publish *Master's Mistress*."

Later, when I asked for permission to use the critique in this book, she asked her new agent if it was okay. After reviewing my critique, her agent, Ellen, said yes and added this:

> "He was spot on with his editorial comments! Did I mention that I hate the overuse of flashbacks too?"

See what you think.

Amoda Ni Cormac tossed three more logs onto the flames before turning to grab the large pot of water to boil. She tensed as she heard heavy footsteps approach. A shudder raced through her and she set the pot down softly.

Amoda gathered her skirts in her hand and tiptoed over to the distant corner of the kitchen. Moving aside the wooden door, she slipped inside the tight crawlspace. She ran her hands over her the goose-prickled flesh of her bare arms and winced as she encountered the bruises from her last beating. She cringed as memories flooded through her. Once more she relived the violence that invaded her nights.

His heavy weight on her chest made her struggles futile. Amoda bucked and twisted under him, finally freeing her hands. She scratched at his face, raking her nails deeply across the weathered skin, drawing blood and curses of pain. All she wanted was to be left alone.

The stench of stale wine and tobacco filled her senses,

drowning her in a sense of helplessness, of desperation and added to her horror. She screamed, her fists pummeling his shoulders, her fingers pulling at his hair, her legs kicking out at him harder as she felt the calloused hand creeping under her tunic, mauling a bare breast.

"Too much for the Prince to handle, I say. What he doesn't know can't trouble him."

Would you turn the page? Any edits needed? Make notes before you read on.

Here is what I told Pat in the flogging critique: The immediate flashback discouraged me. And all those italics!

There is good writing here, and a well-imagined world. I would much rather be plunged into it rather than reliving it. As I've said before, the reader wants to know what's happening now, not then. By the way, the "beating" turns out to be more of a rape, so I wondered why it was called a beating. I believe that, while the writer is working hard to introduce a sympathetic character to us, we're being told something the writer thinks we need to know. Why not start with the beating/rape as an immediate scene rather than history?

My notes:

Amoda Ni Cormac tossed three more logs onto the flames before turning to grab the <u>large</u> pot of water to boil. She tensed ~~as~~ **when** she heard heavy footsteps approach. A shudder raced through her and she set the pot down <u>softly</u>. *(A few nit-picks: "large" is a vague and relative conclusion word, and doesn't actually contribute to a picture. If you want to show that it's large, you could use another way to let the reader understand that. For example, it would be heavy, right? What about:* Amoda Ni Cormac tossed three more logs onto the flames, and then strained to lift the pot of water to boil. *Using adverbs such as "softly" aren't truly descriptive most of the time. I try to avoid them. For example, here she could ease the pot back down, which shows rather than tells. I changed "as" to "when" because she did not tense simultaneously with hearing the footsteps—the sound has to come first.)*

Amoda gathered her skirts ~~in her hand~~ and tiptoed ~~over~~ to the ~~distant~~ corner of the kitchen. ~~Moving aside the wooden door, she slipped inside the tight crawlspace.~~ She ran her hands over her the goose-prickled flesh of her bare arms and winced ~~as~~ **when** she encountered the bruises from her last beating. ~~She cringed as memories flooded through her. Once more she relived the violence that invaded her nights.~~ *(Argh! So we go to a flashback. I wouldn't here. Other things: in my understanding, and in houses today, a crawlspace is beneath the floor of the building. So I don't understand her getting into one here. There are bits of overwriting. For example, when a woman gathers her skirts, by necessity she uses her hands, so adding that bit of detail is just clutter because a reader will automatically imagine the process. In this case, "distant" is also a vague and relative descriptor—it doesn't actually help give a picture of the room. Furthermore, is it actually needed? What does it matter how far away the corner is as long as she hides? I removed the crawlspace and have inserted a transitional element below to avoid a flashback.)*

He stormed in and threw her to the floor. His heavy weight on her chest ~~had~~ made her struggles futile. Amoda ~~had~~ bucked and twisted under him, finally freeing her hands. She scratched at his face, raking her nails deeply across the weathered skin, drawing blood and curses of pain. All she wanted was to be left alone. *(Here I've made the event happen in the now of the story and gotten rid of the italics.)*

The stench of stale wine and tobacco filled her senses, drowning her in a sense of helplessness, of desperation and added to her horror. She screamed~~; her fists~~ **and pummeled** ~~pummeling~~ his shoulders. ~~her fingers pulling at~~ **She pulled his hair** ~~, her legs kicking out~~ **and kicked** at him harder ~~as when she felt the~~ **his** calloused hand ~~creeping~~ **crept** under her tunic~~, mauling a bare~~ and **mauled her** breast. *(Too many "ings" here. And you gave the action to parts of her body rather than her. This is a scene of violent action, and I think that short, active sentences do a better job of delivering the*

experience. "ing" words are softer, and lack the bite and punch of the past tense I substituted. Another thought—since this is a rape, wouldn't he shove his hand under her tunic rather than creep it? IMO.)
"Too much for the Prince to handle, I say. What he doesn't know can't trouble him." *(Could use a dialogue tag here to show who says this.)*

The rest of her pages were similar, with good writing slowed down here and there by bits of overwriting. There was more backstory, which further slowed getting me involved with this girl's story. I suggested Pat look further down the narrative line for a better, more immediate place to start the story.

I liked the work and encouraged Pat to keep at it. I suggested that she look for ways to tighten the narrative, make it crisp and active. And I told her to, above all, get into what's happening now and avoid the past until she had us hooked.

And here's what she did: I looked up her published book and this is what the first manuscript page would now be:

His heavy weight on her chest made her struggles futile. Amoda bucked and twisted under him, finally freeing her hands. She scratched his face, raking her nails deeply across the weathered skin, drawing blood and curses of pain.

The stench of stale wine and sweat filled her senses, drowned her in helplessness, and added to her horror. She screamed. Her fists pummeled his shoulders. She pulled his hair. Desperately, she kicked him as his calloused hand crept under her tunic to maul a bare breast.

"Too much for the Prince to handle, I say. What he doesn't know can't trouble him." Rognvaldr sneered. His hot breath washed over her face and neck, spittle splattering on the bare flesh.

"The King will kill you for this!" She clawed at his bare arms. Her teeth sunk into flesh, biting, ripping until he retreated. Weeping, she curled into a ball as the shadowy figure hobbled out of her chamber. The cold morning air whispered over her torn clothes, caressing her exposed flesh.

Amoda pulled her tunic and apron around her and stood on shaky legs. Sunlight streamed across the floor; a cruel reminder of her misery. Head bent, she hurried out the door to clean up before she began her day's chores.

Amoda Ni Cormac tossed three more logs onto the flames before she strained to lift the pot of water to boil. She tensed when she heard the heavy shuffle of footsteps approach. A shudder raced through her, and she eased the pot down onto the hearth.

Workout 4

THE FIRST SIXTEEN LINES of Syndey's YA fantasy:

Okay, whoever said waiting was fun needs to be taught a lesson in boredom. I sighed in annoyance as my eyes roved over the treetops from my perch in the watchtower. Ardoway had gone hunting as usual, leaving me to get the firewood. That, however, already lay in a heap on the floor. Now all I could do was wait for my brother and hope that he managed to bring down a deer for our dinner tonight. It had been over a month since his last catch, and we desperately needed the meat.

Still, a sigh rushed out of me and I rolled over onto my stomach to straddle one of the rafters. I hate waiting, and I hate not being able to go hunting either. Just because I'm a girl doesn't mean I can't learn to use a bow too! Splinters dug into my palms when I clenched my hands in anger, then I cursed and jerked them away from the beam to pick out the fragmented wood. Great. Bored and in pain. A perfect combination if there ever was one. But when my eyes raked impatiently across the edge of the forest again, they halted. Then grew wide in disbelief.

A deer stood not more than forty paces away from the tower, ears pricked toward the village in the center of the valley. Atop its head, a crown of massive horns reached to the skies. Its fur was lush and thick, body well filled out despite the unceasing winter. And I was stuck here, looking at it and without any means of trying to catch it!

What was your vote? Yes? No? Almost? Go through and edit—there are some needed in the second paragraph.

The voice is good, and the writing as well, though in places there's a bit too much of it for me. Here's a quick line edit to show what I mean.

Splinters dug into my palms ~~when I clenched my hands in anger~~, then I cursed and jerked ~~them~~ away ~~from the beam~~ to pick **them** out ~~the fragmented wood~~. Great. Bored and in pain. A perfect combination if there ever was one. But when ~~my eyes~~ I raked **my gaze** ~~impatiently~~ across the edge of the forest again, ~~they halted. Then~~ my **eyes** grew wide in disbelief.

Even edited, though, there wasn't much tension in this for me, so it got a no vote. Not much of a story question raised, and no suggestion of a problem ahead. Almost all of the chapter that followed, something like fifteen pages, was world-introduction and set-up. While nicely written, it was still exposition with not much happening.

But later in the chapter came something that was compelling. I've adapted some of Sydney's later material to create this possible opening page. What do you think?

Few people passed me on my way to the tiny shack at the edge of the village. Those who lived here often went in the opposite direction, either towards the forest or to home. The only thing beyond was blackened ruins, and then the mountains. It was a foreboding place, especially at night when the wind screamed through the valley like a child that could never be soothed.

Something flickered in the corner of my eye, and I jumped, glancing at the ruins. What . . . It was taboo to go near the burned-out house after the fire.

A hazy outline hovered just above the ground near the ruins. It solidified into a recognizable shape. A woman. She stood an easy six feet in height, and her glowing blue eyes pinned me to the spot. Long, dark hair flowed about her shoulders and her stern but young-looking face bore the faintest trace of a smile. Her skin, nearly transparent, pulsed and faded and a long, pale dress as thin as mist blew about her slender ankles.

My mouth opened and closed several times like a fish's would, trying to find something to say, some sound to make, but it was as if my voice had been rendered clean from me. Thoughts rapid-fired in my mind. A ghost? A spirit? What exactly was she? Was she even real?

"Come." She mouthed, beckoning me with a crook of one long, thin finger.

Then she vanished, blown apart as if by the wind.

This would have definitely grabbed me. Like so many first chapters I read, the writer starts the story too early and focuses on set-up.

But why? If you can engage the reader with something truly interesting happening, there is plenty of time to weave the world in as things continue to happen and story questions are raised. There's just no reason start with set-up when you can start with tension.

Workout 5

Carolyn's first sixteen lines:

A wave of wooziness tells me my blood pressure is dropping. Internal bleeding. It won't be long now. Focus, I think, heading through the crowded restaurant to confront Shady Ben Foley and warn his young companions about him. One good deed at the end of my otherwise useless life. Time slows and details take on a dreamlike clarity: snake charmer music and the spicy smells twine through the air, painted horse heads and bejeweled scabbards decorate the walls, silverware clinks on plates. I'd dragged my boyfriend Cubby into this cheesy Mongolian Restaurant in the course of stalking Foley. My last meal, I think with a rush of grief and terror, nearly tripping over an oriental rug as I avoid colliding with a waiter. It had to come sometime. My condition, known as Vein Star Syndrome, is the proverbial ticking time bomb in the head. Once you're past the point of vascular rupture, no medical attention can save you. Cubby waits back at the table, unaware just how grave my situation has become. I didn't tell him. I didn't want him to stop me from doing this one last decent thing.

"Ben Foley," I say, interrupting their conversation. "Remember me? Pembroke Pines?" I grip the back of an empty chair for support.

Shady Ben gives me this blank look and exchanges bewildered glances with his companions, two blonde men and a pretty girl with long dark ringlets. I remember him so (snip)

Okay, note your verdict and mark up the narrative as needed.

I READ ON

Good story elements, good writing, and an interesting voice got me to turn the page. There's certainly drama evoked in the first paragraph with her anticipation of dying soon, and then the story immediately adds conflict. Nicely done, Carolyn. There are a couple of little things that I should note, and a little tightening.

A wave of wooziness tells me my blood pressure is dropping. Internal bleeding. It won't be long now. Focus, I think, heading through the crowded restaurant to confront Shady Ben Foley and warn his young companions about him. One good deed at the end of my otherwise useless life.

Time slows and details take on a dreamlike clarity: snake charmer music and the spicy smells twine through the air, painted horse heads and bejeweled scabbards decorate the walls, silverware clinks on plates. I'd dragged my boyfriend Cubby into this cheesy Mongolian Restaurant in the course of stalking Foley. My last meal, I think with a rush of grief and terror, nearly tripping over an oriental rug as I avoid colliding with a waiter. It had to come sometime. My condition, known as Vein Star Syndrome, is the proverbial ticking time bomb in the head. Once you're past the point of vascular rupture, no medical attention can save you. Cubby waits back at the table, unaware of just how grave my situation is has become. I ~~didn't tell~~ **hadn't told** him. I didn't want him to stop me from doing this one last decent thing. *(I like description elements such as "twined through the air.")*

"Ben Foley," I say, interrupting their conversation. "Remember me? <u>Pembroke Pines</u>?" I grip the back of an empty chair for support. *(It's not clear whether "Pembroke Pines" is a person's or a place's name. Could be either. Turns out*

her name is Justine. I think it should be included here, e.g.,
"Justine? From Pembroke Pines?")

Shady Ben gives me this blank look and exchanges bewildered glances with his companions, two **blond** ~~blonde~~
men and a pretty girl with long dark ringlets. I remember
him so (snip) *(On "blond:" Common usage is without the*
"e," though using it is still correct. Some use "blond" for
men and "blonde" for women, but I think one consistent
spelling is best.)

There were similar small opportunities for polishing, but
overall it was an opening chapter that made me want chapter
two. Thanks, Carolyn.

Workout 6

Kim's first sixteen lines:

Michelle Evans burst into SecuraCorp's conference room. "You all need to see this right away."

Blake Barnett didn't have a chance to say a word, let alone stop his cyclone-like secretary from interrupting their Monday, 8 a.m. meeting. He looked across the table at his business partner, Mike Jacobs, sipping a cup of coffee.

Mike grinned and shrugged, as if to say, 'Hey, you hired her pal'.

Blake rose from his chair. "Michelle, we're trying to—"

"Blake, they have someone named Angel."

Mike jumped up. "What?" Coffee sloshed out of his cup and onto the walnut-veneer boardroom table.

Her words took a few seconds to register in Blake's

head. Angel, the world's first cloned human? Impossible.

"That can't be."

"It's true. This arrived special delivery." She handed

him a disc enclosed in a clear plastic case.

He snatched what appeared to be a DVD from her hand,

and powered up his laptop. "Michelle, would you leave us

alone, please?"

Almost? No? Yes? Vote and then make notes on what's right or wrong or how it can be edited to work better.

This had virtues, but didn't compel me.

Virtues include starting with a scene and an effort to create tension and raise story questions. But (remember, this is subjective) what happens here didn't grip me or make me really curious about what would happen next.

Parts of the problem include some overwriting and a clarity question. Allow me to get picky in the interests of adding impact. It needs a lot of work; see if you spotted the same things I did.

Michelle Evans burst into SecuraCorp's conference room. "You all need to see this right away." *(Later we learn that she carries something with urgent information on it. Why not get to it now? "This" has no antecedent and doesn't give a clue that speaks of importance or jeopardy—it's meaningless to the reader, so why include it? It's an information question.)*

Blake Barnett ~~didn't have a chance to say a word~~, let alone stop his cyclone-like secretary from interrupting their ~~Monday, 8 a.m.~~ meeting. He looked across the table at ~~his business partner,~~ Mike Jacobs, sipping **his** ~~a cup of~~ coffee. *(While I appreciate an effort to characterize the secretary, just how well does this narrative really work? For example, Blake "didn't have a chance to say a word." Actually, he does. She stops speaking. He looks across the table. A sentence from now, he'll stand and say something. So this statement doesn't reflect any kind of reality. I also think this is over-detailed: we don't need to know that this is their 8 o'clock meeting. We don't need to know at this moment that Mike is his business partner, nor that he's sipping coffee (by the way, he's not sipping "a cup of coffee," he's just sipping coffee—a whole cup is one helluva sip). There's information and detail here that doesn't advance the story and, for me, slows things down.)*

~~Mike grinned and shrugged as if to say, 'Hey, you hired her, pal'.~~ *(Now, this really slows things down, and sure doesn't contribute to a sense of urgency, IMO. I'd cut it all.)*

Blake **stood** ~~rose from his chair.~~ "Michelle, we're trying to—" *(I suggest "stood" instead of "rose from his chair," which could also mean that he levitated. "Stood" is a nice, specific verb that gives an instant picture. In addition, why are we stalling with Blake's protest?)*

"Blake, they have someone named Angel." *(Now we're getting somewhere—but where? This is still withholding from the reader, an information question, and vague. It even uses a vague word, "someone." If the secretary knows enough to tell that whatever it is she holds is urgent, then she knows enough to be specific here.)*

Mike jumped up. "What?" ~~Coffee sloshed out of his cup and onto the walnut-veneer boardroom table.~~ *(You know what I'm going to say, don't you? We don't need to know that the table is "walnut-veneer boardroom." Yes, he jumped up in reaction to her vague announcement. But did we need to slosh coffee? More detail that doesn't contribute to showing us something compelling, in my view.)*

Her words <u>took a few seconds to register</u> in Blake's head. Angel, the world's first cloned human? Impossible. "That can't be." *(Why would the words take a few seconds to register? As we learn later, he was intimately involved in rescuing this cloned girl, so his reaction should have been immediate. More than that, the world's first cloned human is definitely interesting information, yet we don't get to it until now.)*

"It's true. This arrived special delivery." She handed him a **DVD** ~~disc enclosed in a clear plastic case~~. *(More ineffective narrative. If she knows what's on the "disc enclosed in a clear plastic case," then why the heck didn't she say so* *up front instead of all this dancing around? As for "disc enclosed in a clear plastic case," this is cautious over-explaining. She knows it's a DVD—she has to have viewed it to know what's on it—so why not have her say what it is?)*

He snatched **it** ~~what appeared to be a DVD~~ from her ~~hand~~ and powered up his laptop. "Michelle, would you leave us alone, please?" *(As just pointed out, we should already know that this is a DVD. The "what appeared" is more cautious description. Why does he ask to be alone if she already knows what's on the DVD? This opening to a thriller/suspense novel needs to let 'er rip, not dance around. In my view, that is.)*

The story that develops could be interesting, but the delivery continued to need work, with more detail than needed and some info-dumping. How could this opening have been stronger? Here's a quick rewrite:

Blake Barnett's secretary burst into the meeting. "Angel's been kidnapped." Michelle handed him a disk in a case. "This DVD just came."

Blake said, "Dammit!" Even though people tended to think of the first human clone as an object, Angel was just a little girl with big, sad eyes. He loaded the disk in his laptop while his partner Mike hurried around the table.

Now we have the clone aspect in, plus a strong hint that he has a connection with her. I hope this illustrates how Kim could have spent her narrative hooking me on the drama of her story instead of filling me in on tabletops and coffee spills. And this version took only five lines of manuscript narrative, leaving lots of room to further hook the reader into a story about a kidnapped clone.

Workout 7

THE FIRST SIXTEEN LINES of Greg's fantasy novel:

To tell the truth, Dora Faye didn't know whether she was about to kill herself or not. All her life she'd wanted to be spontaneous and creative, open to all the sweetly surprising spin-on-the-head-of-a-pin possibilities of life — especially now with regards to the ending of it — and tonight she figured she'd just go with the flow. Live or die, oh me oh my. Maybe yes, maybe no. Easy come, easy go. Tra la la la la. But one thing was for damn sure. She wanted a corndog. The carnival was in town.

On this sticky June night her mind played tricks on her. Snowflakes danced over the Ferris wheel. Since snowflakes don't have a mind of their own to zig and zag, flit and flap independently, this made no sense at all to Dora Faye. Snow

in June?

Her nostrils flared as a frypit breeze of onions and pep-

pers—greasy with diesel fumes—teased her brunette hair.

She'd chopped it to try for a more youthful image before they

snipped her American Express; suddenly lacking the plastic

cash for the nip 'n' tucks to firm up the face, the pageboy

thing just wasn't working at all for her.

As she drove her Delta 88 ragtop into the parking lot

and killed the ignition, her ears caught a muddy wave of pop

tunes, punched out by worn-out carny speakers, as they and

her Top 40 regrets washed through her mind.

Page turn? Notes for this writer?

Opening and voice moved me on

Nice voice here, and fun writing for the most part. I did read on, and have a note later for Greg about that. This opening, thanks to the first paragraph, raises a strong story question. Some notes:

~~To tell the truth,~~ Dora Faye didn't know whether she was about to kill herself or not. All her life she'd wanted to be spontaneous and creative, open to all the sweetly surprising spin-on-the-head-of-a-pin possibilities of life—especially now with regards to the ending of it—and tonight she figured she'd just go with the flow. Live or die, oh me oh my. Maybe yes, maybe no. Easy come, easy go. Tra la la la la. But one thing was for damn sure. She wanted a corndog. ~~The carnival was in town.~~ *(Except for the first phrase, I really liked this. The contrast between the death wish and the corn dog craving was engaging. I cut the "truth" phrase because it seems a shame to begin such an interesting piece of narrative with a tired old phrase. Wasn't needed, either, IMO. I cut the line about the carnival because the corndog was such a surprise and nifty ending for the paragraph. I've added the carnival later.)*

~~On this sticky June night her mind played tricks on her.~~ Snowflakes danced over the **carnival** Ferris wheel. Since snowflakes ~~don't~~ **didn't** have a mind of their own to zig and zag, flit and flap independently, ~~this~~ **that** made no sense at all to Dora Faye. Snow **on a sticky June night** ~~in June~~? *(The first sentence steps out of her point of view and into the author's. In a deep third person POV, she wouldn't be thinking about a sticky June night in this way. And "her mind played tricks on her" is telling rather than showing. Thought-starter: begin with the snowflakes part. Then, in-*

stead of the "Snow in June" internal monologue, carry on with the no sense thing at the end to describe the night, i.e., Neither did snowflakes on a sticky June night.)

Her nostrils flared ~~as~~ **when** a fry-pit breeze of onions and peppers—greasy with diesel fumes—teased her ~~bru-~~ ~~nette~~ hair. She'd chopped it to try for a more youthful image before they snipped her American Express; ~~suddenly~~ lacking the plastic cash for the nip-'n'-tucks to firm up the face, the pageboy thing just wasn't working at all for her. *(Stating the color of her hair is another slip in POV—unless she's looking at it in a mirror (a rear-view mirror, in this case), she wouldn't be thinking about the color. I liked the "fry-pit breeze" part, but that leads to an inconsistency in the next paragraph. I think this description could be cut or moved to later.)*

~~As~~ **After** she drove her Delta 88 ragtop into the parking lot and killed the ignition, ~~her ears~~ she caught a muddy wave of pop tunes, punched out by worn-out carny speakers as ~~they and~~ her Top 40 regrets washed through her mind. *(This may be totally subjective, but . . . while "ragtop" is a good synonym for convertible, it created an image of a convertible with the top up (because of "top"). Turns out the top is down. "Convertible" would have left the position of the top open. Or it could have been showing with something like:* Wind tossing her hair, she drove her Delta 88 ragtop into the parking lot and killed the ignition. She caught . . . *And let's not have her ears doing the catching of songs, let's have her do it.*

Here's a staging problem: in the previous paragraph, before we know she's in a convertible with the top down, she smells odors on the breeze. Yet at that point she isn't in the parking lot by the carnival, as we learn here. Rethink the order of things here. I'd get her into the parking lot first, stop the car, and then let the breeze do its thing. And if she's driving, the air flow of a top-down convertible would defeat any breeze.)

Good stuff to develop further.

Workout 8

ALYSSA'S FIRST SIXTEEN LINES:

When I met Isabeau, I thought it was just another ordinary day. Though I suppose you can say that about any day that unexpectedly rips your life apart.

The last bell had rung, and I was trying to figure out my homework schedule as I walked across the parking lot. I couldn't decide if I should study for my chemistry test before, during, or after writing that 5-page paper about Macbeth and doing those 45 trig problems and... there she was. Leaning against my junker of a car, and tapping her fingers rhythmically on the hood. The sun painted the waves in her burnt red hair with streaks of gold, and her clothes – jeans and a sleeveless high-necked shirt – showed off her athletic figure.

My first thought? *Wow, she's gorgeous.* I never said it was a brilliant thought, just that it was my first one.

I cleared my throat. "C-Can I help you?" Lame, I admit, but I didn't have a lot of experience talking to beautiful girls. Or any girls, really.

Her eyes locked onto mine with an electric jolt. They weren't blue or green or hazel or brown or violet – they were all of those at once, encircling her pupils with slivers of color that spiraled into her soul. "What did they call you?"

My brain did a double-check. Yep, it had heard her right. "Excuse me? What did who call me?"

What, if anything, do you think this writer should have done differently?

ALMOST

The voice is inviting. Its confidence suggests that I'm in the hands of a good storyteller. The protagonist was immediately likeable to me as well. There's a story question raised—what will happen between this guy and this girl—but so what? There's not much energy or intensity or "size" to the story question. It's on the ordinary side. She's beautiful, but that doesn't do it for me.

But the rest of the chapter was charming and continued to raise the level of that story question and add others. But how to get that first page turned?

Well, I've cobbled together bits of later narrative and below is a roughed-out alternative. To make room, I decided that some things just weren't important enough for the first page:

- The foreshadowing first paragraph, an attempt to create enough tension to get me to turn the page. I'd rather be swept into the story than told about what's coming.
- The laundry list of things he has to study. While that paragraph is great for setting the scene and characterizing, it can be shorter.
- The extensive description of the girl didn't seem all needed to me.

So below is some of the current first page trimmed down and an attempt to raise the intensity of the story question through the use of characterization rather than events. To be fair to the way the chapter is written, it seemed harsh to try to jam an action story question onto the first page, but I found the girl's character to be quite compelling, so this is a try to crank up the interest via her. See what you think.

The last bell had rung, and I was trying to figure out my homework schedule as I walked across the parking lot. Should I study for my chemistry test before, during, or after writing that five-page Macbeth paper, or—

And there she was. Leaning against my junker of a car, tapping her fingers on the hood. The sun painted the waves in her burnt red hair with streaks of gold.

"C-Can I help you?" Lame, I admit, but I didn't have a lot of experience talking to beautiful girls. Or any girls, really.

Her eyes locked onto mine with an electric jolt. They weren't blue or green or hazel or brown or violet—they were all of those at once, encircling her pupils with slivers of color that spiraled into her soul. She said, "You don't look like a Christopher Smith."

What? I shrugged. "Yeah, I get that a lot. My father's American, but my mother's Japanese. I know I take after her side, but—"

She held up her hand. "Not what I meant. I know from my research on twenty-first century America that its melting pot culture allowed for people of differing ethnic appearances to have names of seemingly divergent derivation. I was referring to the names themselves: Christopher, from the Greek name Christophoros, combining Christos or Christ with phero, meaning to bear or carry. Thus, 'bearing Christ.' Then you have Smith, deriving from the word smitan, meaning 'to smite,' (snip)

Now, that's an unusual character and fresh writing, and I wanted to know more.

Workout 9

ERIKA'S FIRST PAGE:

I hadn't dressed for running and was losing ground fast.

The shiny black dress shoes I wore burrowed into the dry

sand with every step, my tuxedo jacket flapped open as I

pumped my arms. The San Diego evening was cooler than

you'd expect, brisk gusts of wind bouncing off the sea at

sporadic intervals. A full moon blazed out of a cloudless,

starry sky, washing the beach in cool shades of blue.

Waves sent salty spray into my face as I reached back

to tear the jacket off my shoulders and fling it to the sand

behind me. My quarry raced on ahead, lighter than me and

almost dancing across the top of the sand. If I had to guess,

I'd say I was chasing a woman, 5' 1" max, with a body fat

percentage that had to be in the low teens. She wore an all-black ensemble, complete with a matching ski mask and boots that kicked up little spits of sand with each stride.

Her speed was impressive; she widened the gap between us by almost two paces for each one I took. She ran like someone who knew where she was going, my guess was that she was headed toward the public parking lot a quarter mile ahead. I had to assume she'd prepared a contingency plan in that parking lot somewhere. Guns, explosives, sharp rocks, something painful of that nature. If I didn't catch up with her before she reached her defense cache, I was guessing I wouldn't like the welcome.

"Enough of this crap," I said and stopped just long enough to kick off my dress shoes. A (snip)

Vote, and then go through and edit. This opening is burdened with overwriting—draw lines through words you would cut and note what you would replace them with. That's what I'll do in the edit that follows. But first, my verdict.

Yes, but . . .

Ah, a good strong action scene with clear writing and a good (though over-written at times) voice. The scene is well set, what's happening is clear, and good story questions are raised: what did the quarry do, who/what is the person chasing her, and why. But the narrative should be crisper, though, and my belief is that you can't waste the space it takes for verbiage that should be subjected to the delete key. Still, I turned the page, but would have done so more convinced that I was in good hands with some editing, which I'm sure Erika can do. Notes to that effect:

I hadn't dressed for running and was losing ground fast. ~~The shiny black~~ **My** dress shoes burrowed into the dry sand with every step, my tuxedo jacket flapped open as I pumped my arms. The San Diego evening was cooler than you'd expect, brisk gusts of wind bouncing off the sea at sporadic intervals. A full moon blazed out of a cloudless, starry sky, washing the beach in cool shades of blue.

Waves sent salty spray into my face as I ~~reached back to tear~~ **tore** the jacket off ~~my shoulders~~ and ~~fling~~ **flung** it to the sand ~~behind me~~. My quarry raced on ahead, ~~lighter than me and~~ almost dancing across the top of the sand. ~~If I had to guess, I'd say~~ **I guessed** I was chasing a woman, 5' 1" max, with a body fat percentage that had to be in the low teens. She wore an all-black ensemble, complete with a matching ski mask and boots that kicked up little spits of sand with each stride. *(I like "little spits of sand"—nice description, very visual, promises more good writing ahead.)*

Her speed was impressive; she widened the gap between us by almost two paces for each one I took. She ran like someone who knew where she was going, my guess was that she was headed toward the ~~public~~ parking lot a quarter mile ahead. I had to assume she'd prepared a contingency plan **there** ~~in that parking lot somewhere~~. Guns, explosives, sharp rocks, something painful ~~of that nature~~. If I didn't catch up with her before she reached her defense cache, I was guessing I wouldn't like the welcome. *(A lot of use of "guessing" and "guess" here. Look for alternatives (figured, etc.) or delete some, too much repetition.)*

"Enough of this crap," I said and stopped just long enough to kick off my ~~dress~~ shoes. A (snip) *(We already know they are dress shoes, no need to repeat.)*

Workout 10

EDI'S FIRST PAGE:

"Eugenia, get away from that man!" She's only eight, and the Blessed Mother knows what he might be saying to her. I cannot let her out of my sight for one minute on this street.

Eugenia doesn't hear me; too many carriages rolling by. The man puts his hand on her head, and she stands there like she's in church with the priest blessing her. I force myself to get up, though I feel like hunger has pinned me to this corner of the sidewalk forever. I can't let him touch her like that.

"Eugenia!" I put all my strength into the word. The man hands her something, and she runs back to me. Thank goodness, I can sit back down and put my back against the bricks, out of the wind. She stands in front of me. What a little scarecrow, with her arms straight out, flapping, all excited."Ligia, read this for me!"

I take the sheet of paper and spell out the first line to myself, in my head. I'm glad I did. Eugenia mustn't know what this says. I frown and look up at her. "What did he say to you?" She looks scared, like my voice is going to whip her or something.

"Nothing, Ligia. I mean, he said I should read this if I ever need a home, or a bed, or some parents to look after me. He wasn't like the police. Honest, Ligia."

"He's not the police," I said. "He's something worse. He was trying to con you." I try to make my voice sad and threatening at the same time. "There are people who steal children."

Vote, please, and then add your notes. Where could this be stronger?

I DID TURN THE PAGE, BUT . . .

An inviting voice and strong, clear writing served to draw me in. The way the period nature of the piece is introduced by the carriages rolling by and the way her hunger and the cold are woven in are excellent. But I think it could be stronger in two places. As often happens, there was material on the second page that would make the first page stronger. Also, I think it would be best if the reader learns on this first page that Ligia is twelve years old. Maybe there's a graceful way in the third or fourth paragraph if the description is trimmed a little. Notes:

"Eugenia, get away from that man!" She's only eight, and the Blessed Mother knows what he might be saying to her. I cannot let her out of my sight for one minute on this street.

~~Eugenia~~ **She** doesn't hear me; too many carriages rolling by. The man puts his hand on her head, and she stands there like she's in church with the priest blessing her. I force myself to get up, though I feel like hunger has pinned me to this corner of the sidewalk forever. I can't let him touch her like that.

"Eugenia!" I put all my strength into the word. The man hands her something, and she runs back to me. Thank goodness, I can sit back down and put my back against the bricks, out of the wind. She stands in front of me. What a little scarecrow, with her arms straight out, flapping, all excited. "Ligia, read this for me!" (*Love the description of Eugenia.*)

I take the sheet of paper and spell out the first line to myself, in my head. I'm glad I did. Eugenia mustn't know what this says. I frown and look up at her. "What did he say to you?" She looks scared, like my voice is going to whip her or something. (*For me, this would be stronger if we knew what the note said. Why hold it back if it's a part of the world they live in and it really is a threat of some kind? So show us what disturbs her. You can take out some of the description to make room.)*

"Nothing, Ligia. I mean, he said I should read this if I ever need a home, or a bed, or some parents to look after me. He wasn't like the police. Honest, Ligia."

"He's not the police," I said. ~~"He's something worse. He was trying to con you." I try to make my voice sad and threatening at the same time.~~ **"There are people who steal children. They promise to put you on a train and send you out of the city, to a home where someone will love you and take care (snip)** *(I've substituted the text from the next page. For me, it tells me more about the trouble these children are in.)*

Workout 11

JACK'S FIRST PAGE:

The story of how my sister took over the world probably starts with a brawl in a bar, eighty years ago. Not a brawl my sister was involved in, naturally, for she was only nine years old at the time. But Moira was the reason I was there, in that bar, and my being there is why Yvonne Lambert was there.

To tell you about Moira, I have to tell you Yvonne's story, too. And not just because it was Yvonne who started the brawl. And not just because Yvonne and I fell in love.

This meeting in the bar, followed by the brawl, was my and Yvonne's first date. We called it that after we were together, anyway, both appreciating the irony of a "first date" that resulted in minor injuries, a night in jail and my banishment from civilization.

It was on Aldrin, specifically its inland mountain resort town Montessecchi. Yvonne had a spacecraft she was willing to hire out for twelve months. So were a lot of other people with spacecraft, but this trip would be hell and gone from anyplace else, and would also be illegal. From what little I knew of her before we met—reputation algorithm, her vid advertising her ship for hire—Yvonne seemed like she would be open to the idea. In fact, I half expected her to be enthusiastic about it. The illegal part, at least.

Aldrin back then was a lot like it is now: a vacation destination for the filthy rich. Its reason for being was its four spectacular resorts, attracting a wealthy transient population.

What's your vote? Is this okay as it is? Should the author do anything to give it a stronger hook?

A big Yes for me.

I've included this narrative to show you a first page that is, in my view, practically perfect in every way despite the fact that it doesn't do a number of things that are in the first-page checklist: What Jack didn't do:

- ~~Something is happening. This does NOT include a character musing about whatever.~~
- ~~What happens is dramatized in an immediate scene with action and description plus, if it works, dialogue.~~
- ~~The protagonist does something.~~
- ~~It happens in the NOW of the story.~~
- ~~Backstory? What backstory? We're in the NOW of the story.~~
- ~~Set-up? What set-up? We're in the NOW of the story.~~

The voice and the many story questions raised in all but the last paragraph are what did it for me—I'm sure there are folks who will disagree, reading being as subjective as you can get.

I said "practically perfect." The one thing I would change is the last paragraph. It signals the beginning of set-up exposition, and it was information that could—and should—have waited. I would have jumped ahead to a paragraph on the second page that got deeper into the scene this way:

The bar was a lot darker on the inside than out and brimming with loud, rough people just off work. The place smelled like peanut shells and body odor. You couldn't walk five feet without having to maneuver around somebody.

Thanks

I THANK YOU, THANK YOU, THANK YOU for buying/reading my book, and I hope some aspect of it will inform your writing and help you lift it a notch or two.

How about a review? If you feel you profited from this book, I would appreciate your posting a review on Internet sites such as Amazon.com and BN.com (Barnes & Noble).

Bottom, line, I want to help writers whether I'm compensated or not. Feel free to contact me through my website at crrreative. com.

Here's how I sign this book:

> Write!
> Rewrite!
> Enjoy!

All best,

Ray

B. C. WRITER   by Ray Rhamey

Cave editor.

About the author

As it turns out, storytelling has pretty much become my life. As a boy, when I read the *Book of Knowledge* the short stories and novellas were always the most fascinating parts. When I teened, I moved on to science fiction and fantasy via magazines such as *Analog* and *If* and a galaxy of mass market paperback books. SF and fantasy have been a constant in my reading ever since, although thrillers are my mainstay these days.

I also consumed comic books by the bale, which led to a desire to be a cartoonist—not in the sense of a style of art, but as a creator of drawn stories. As an adult, I created a couple of comic strips in hopes of becoming a professional cartoonist. Came close with one, but it wasn't to be (yet—there's a graphic novel growing in my mind, the opening of which I used as an example of bridging conflict on page 205; Hamilton is a pig.). Some of the cartoons in this book are mine.

As an advertising copywriter and then creative director (read: "editor") for twenty or so years, most of my seventy produced commercials were thirty-second stories, with beginnings, middles, and ends. My adverstorytelling propelled me to the top tier of the Chicago advertising scene.

While in advertising, another form of storytelling called to me: screenwriting. I left Chicago advertising to tackle screenwriting in Los Angeles and studied the craft in books, at UCLA, and at the American Film Institute. A few speculative screenplays later, I signed with an agent. But, while I could craft screen stories in a professional way, I never came up with a story that anyone wanted to invest millions in producing.

However, a two-minute animated Cap'n Crunch commercial from my advertising days that was, you guessed it, a story, helped me land a scriptwriting job at Filmation, one of the top Hollywood animation studios at the time. I became a story editor, writing scripts and editing the work of others. The series I worked on was comedy, and it was great fun to chuckle all day at the office. I have twenty half-hour screenplay credits from that gig. During that time, I also scripted a video adaptation of *The Little Engine that Could* for Universal Pictures—it's on the shelves in video stores.

But I moved on from that place and that job, re-entered advertising, ran into ageism, and began reinventing myself as an editor. Starting as a subcontractor for an online editing service, I edited beginner novels, and I became a member of the Editorial Freelancers Association and the Northwest Independent Editors Guild. I launched an online editing service in 2001.

As a form of guerilla marketing to generate editing work, in 2004 I started *Flogging the Quill*, a blog about the art and craft of storytelling. FtQ has become a popular "litblog" on the Internet: thousands of writers stop by every week for my coaching, essays on craft and storytelling, and critiques of writing.

My editing career expanded when I became the content editor for Washington State University's main website. That post evolved into becoming director of video services and creating award-winning videos for the university.

While editing work has come to me as a result of the blog, the most satisfying part has been helping other writers conquer writing difficulties—you should see the delight in the thank-you notes I receive. I've also used the litblog as a springboard to doing workshops focused on storytelling at writer's conferences. More on that later.

My education as a writer and editor includes:

- Bachelor of science and master's in psychology
- Years of on-the-job learning at top advertising agencies
- On-the-job learning as a story editor in film
- Courses in script analysis and screenwriting at the American Film Institute
- The absorption of a gazillion books on the craft of writing novels and screenplays

AND THEN THERE'S THE NOVELIST SIDE OF ME

I've completed five novels, learning as I go. A couple of them were viable enough to land a literary agent.

In terms of focus, I guess "commercial fiction" is mine, although I haven't settled into a single genre. And, so far, my work doesn't precisely conform to the expectations of genre fiction— I've been called a "genre-bender." As best as I can label them, as of this writing my stories are:

- A speculative political thriller, *Gundown (a relaunch of* We the Enemy *due out, as of this writing, in 2015)*
- A murder mystery set in the Old West (out of print)
- A 1950s coming-of-age story with a mystery sub-plot, *The Summer Boy*
- A literary fantasy, set in contemporary America, which could also be considered a speculative thriller, *Hiding Magic (a relaunch of* Finding Magic *due, as of this writing, in 2015 if I get a sequel written)*
- A satirical, tongue-in-cheek riff on the vampire myth, *The Vampire Kitty-cat Chronicles (as of this writing a sequel,* The Hollywood Unmurders, *is planned for 2015)*

I've self-published four of those novels. In the process, I got into book design. A small publisher saw one of my books and liked the work. The company asked me to design for them, and thus was launched a new facet of what I do, the design of book covers and interiors. I'm now the designer for the publisher and for "Indie authors" who publish novels and memoirs.

I don't know where my writing will venture next. I hope to make the time for my graphic novel, working title "Splat!" You can sample my books at rayrhamey.com.

WEBSITES:
- Blog: floggingthequill.com
- Editing and book design services: crrreative.com
- My books: rayrhamey.com

The most helpful writing books on my bookshelves:
- *Story*, Robert McKee
- *On Writing*, Stephen King
- *Stein on Writing*, Sol Stein
- *Writing the Breakout Novel*, Donald Maass
- *Self-Editing for Fiction Writers*, Renni Browne and Dave King

WORKSHOPS
Since 2006 I've been teaching workshops at writers' conferences. It's work I love to do. Current titles are:
- Crafting a Killer First Page
- 3 Keys to Killer Storytelling
- Killer Book Covers for Less than $50
- Creating Killer Description and Dialogue

At this writing I'm also working on a new one that deals with self-editing.

EDITING SERVICES
I offer what I call "story editing," an editing approach that's a

blend of "line" editing and "substantive or developmental" editing. I'm not a copyeditor, although I will catch the huge majority of grammatical and punctuation shortcomings. My strengths are in story and narrative craft. You can check me out at crrreative.com

BOOK DESIGN SERVICES

I don't use templates like outfits such as CreateSpace do; my work is all original and derives from the work itself. More than that, it's personal—at the big companies you aren't in direct contact with the designer.

With me, authors share their ideas and I work with them as well as coming up with new concepts on my own. I don't stop creating concepts until we are both satisfied that we've nailed it. I create covers and the interiors for print books and ebooks (Kindle and epub).

SELF-PUBLISHING HELP

I also help my book design clients set up accounts and get their work published as print and ebooks that sell on Amazon, Barnes & Noble, Kobo, Apple, and other Internet vendors. When you combine all of my services they become an Indie-publishing package to help authors get their books to readers.

Index

CPSIA information can be obtained
at www.ICGtesting.com
Printed in the USA
FFOW01n0918110217
32252FF